THE RIGHT TRACK RETIREMENT

A Simple Planning Strategy to Help You Reduce Risk, Build Income, and Provide Peace of Mind

By Brian P. Quaranta

This book discusses general concepts for retirement income planning and is not intended to provide tax or legal advice. Individuals are urged to consult with their tax and legal professionals regarding these issues.

The stories and characters in this book are fictional. Each story combines facts and circumstances redacted to highlight the subject matter of each chapter. Facts and circumstances are fictional and do not represent any one client in part or in whole. They are included as an educational tool. No story should be treated to apply to the reader's individual circumstances. Always consult with your tax professional, attorney, and advisor before taking any action.

Copyright © 2022 by Brian P. Quaranta. Co-authored and edited by Carol Jean Butler. All rights reserved. No part of this publication may be reproduced, distributed, or transmitted in any form or by any means, electronic or mechanical, including photocopying, recording, or by any information storage and retrieval system, without written permission of the publisher, except in the case of brief quotations embodied in critical reviews and certain other noncommercial uses permitted by copyright law.

Printed in the United States of America

First Printing, 2022

Cover and interior design by the Magellan Creative Team

TABLE OF CONTENTS

INTRODUCTION: WHY HASN'T ANYBODY TOLD ME THIS? i

CHAPTER ONE: INVESTMENT PLAN VS. RETIREMENT PLAN WHICH DO YOU NEED? 1

CHAPTER TWO: THINK LIKE A PENSIONER, NOT A GAMBLER 15

CHAPTER THREE: LEVERAGE THE POWER OF A TWO-BUCKET STRATEGY 27

CHAPTER FOUR: PROTECT YOURSELF FROM BIG MARKET SWINGS 43

CHAPTER FIVE: USE THE NEW TECHNOLOGY TO PROFIT FROM MARKET RETURNS 57

CHAPTER SIX: HOW TO BREAK UP WITH YOUR ADVISOR 69

ABOUT THE AUTHOR 83

GLOSSARY OF TERMS 85

INTRODUCTION

WHY HASN'T ANYBODY TOLD ME THIS?

"If you don't know where you're going, you might wind up someplace else."

~Yogi Berra

My first day on the job at the brokerage firm and phones were ringing off the hook—men with ties loosened and cuffs rolled back were animated and tense, and I could hear yelling coming from the voices on the other ends of the phones. The dot.com bubble had burst and people were losing money left and right. I followed my boss through the turmoil to my little cubicle in a corner against a wall.

"Here you go," my boss smiled and gestured. There sat my desk with a computer and a telephone. "As a junior advisor," he said, "your job here today is to answer these calls"

Right away my phone started ringing. My 22-year-old eyes grew wide. I had just graduated from college and passed my exams. The year was 2000. I had no idea what to tell these people.

"What do I say?" I managed to squeak.

"Remind them not to worry," he said. "It's just a paper loss. You know this stuff, Brian." He patted my back. "They're in it for the long haul."

Oh-kay. I sat down. I answered the calls.

These people were upset—and I mean really angry. I could feel the terror coming through the phone. They wanted out of the market and they wanted me to help them do that, but I was a good soldier and I did as I was told. "It's just a paper loss," I told them. "Remember, you're in it for the long haul."

I repeated these phrases and said them over and over as if that alone would make them true. That terrible year was then followed by the 9/11 terrorist attack, the Enron scandal, and the wars in Afghanistan and Iraq. Still, I got on the phone and told people, "It's just a paper loss, you're in it for the long haul."

It was a 75-year-old man named Jim who woke me up to reality. I'll never forget the day.

"Jim," I said as I had been told to say, "you're in it for the long haul."

"Brian," he said to me, "I'm 75-years old. How much long haul do you think I have left?"

And it hit me. He was right.

I realized in that very moment that it's not a question of whether the market comes back; it's a question of when. *Will the market come back when you need it to?* For all the people who are 10 or fewer years away from retirement, and for people who are in retirement and relying on this money for their income, there might not be time enough to make back what you lost.

The birth of the 401(k) has changed everything about the way we retire. What was once provided for you is now your responsibility. What was once simple has now become complicated. Instead of retiring with a pension and an income, you're retiring with a 401(k) and investments. Retirement accounts are invested 100 percent in market risk, which means you need 100 percent cooperation from the market, or you could run out of money before you run out of life.

How many of you reading this have heard advisors tell you, "Don't worry, hang on, it's only a paper loss?" Does it feel like a paper loss to you?

My name is Brian Quaranta, and I got into the business of financial planning during one of the worst decades on Wall

Street, but it taught me something about the proper way to treat this money. It's the reason why I founded my firm, Secure Money Advisors, and why I'm the host of the radio and television segments *On the Money with Secure Money*. There are wealth-building strategies out there that no one is telling you about. There are things you can do to limit the loss.

I'm here to share these strategies with you without all the bullshit.

The Dirty Secret on Wall Street Nobody Is Talking About

This is how the script is supposed to go: "Mr. and Mrs. Investor, as we see the environment change, we'll make allocation shifts and re-diversify your portfolio so you'll always be in the right asset classes." And Mr. and Mrs. Investor smile and nod their heads. They understand something about the strategy. It relies on bonds to serve as a buffer against risk that according to asset allocation models will protect them from volatility. The pie chart and colorful graphs make it all look pretty great.

But what really happens when the market drops? What really happens when Mr. and Mrs. Investor go to retire? That, my friends, is an entirely different picture.

As a junior advisor—which is just a nice name for "hey kid, can you get me some coffee"—I sat in on hundreds of these meetings. I listened to advisors with 25 years more experience than me talk about these supposedly well-diversified plans. And guess what happened in 2001 to every single person in one of those supposedly well-diversified portfolios designed to protect their money?

They lost. Their account values went down! And the investor at or nearing retirement didn't have time to make up for the loss. People were angry and upset because they were losing money, and they didn't understand why.

I am here to tell you why.

Financial advisors employed by major firms can't deliver on their promise of a protection allocation shift even if they wanted to because of certain regulations in place. These regulations were designed to protect the investor, but for the person nearing retirement, they actually have the unintended side effect of working against you. Here's why:

Your average advisor is managing the portfolios of dozens of clients. When the market drops, he's not sitting there on the phone, selling and trading, getting you in and out of funds. He has too many clients to be able to do that! By law, if he goes into those portfolios and starts trading off all these shares, that's called churning, and it's going to send off a red flag. He could lose his license, lose his job. And second, there's the little-talked-about SEC rule known as 35d-1. This rule applies specifically to mutual funds, and as the language in the prospectus states, a fund must invest at least 80 percent of its assets in the type of investment implied by the fund name.[1] This means that even if the funds in that asset class are tanking, your broker or fund manager can't do a damn thing.

Don't feel bad if you didn't know this. I didn't know this! Before my experience working at that firm, I thought money managers were the good guys doing what the name implies: I thought they were moving you in and out of funds, buying and selling on your behalf. I thought they were managing the money! What I learned is that fund managers and brokers tend to be more interested in seeking out their next client than taking care of the ones they have. You're more likely to find them out on the golf course than on the phone. Because here's the dirty secret on Wall Street that nobody is talking about:

Most retirement portfolios are managed using a passive buy-and-hold strategy. Investors benefit from the gains that average out over time from the market highs and lows—and you know this because this is how your retirement account grows. **But this strategy only works when you have a long period of time.** If you

---

[1] U.S. Securities and Exchange Commission. Frequently Asked Questions about Rule 35d-1 (Investment Company Names) https://www.sec.gov/divisions/investment/guidance/rule35d-1faq.htm Accessed 11/15/2021.

have a shorter timeframe before you need the money like my friend Jim, then a passive investing strategy is not your friend. This is why people were angry, frustrated, and confused. And this is why the problem persists. As you enter or near retirement, you shouldn't be relying on passive investment strategies unless you can afford to lose—but don't worry, because I'm here to show that other strategies exist.

Why Isn't Everybody Doing This? Part 1

After that experience, I considered getting out of the industry. Even if I started my own firm, I didn't know how to do things differently, and so I was uncertain about how to move forward with my career. The year was 2006, and I had gotten an invitation to attend a seminar. I put that invitation in my FranklinCovey planner—which was pretty empty those days—and drove home to New Jersey to visit with my family. I was still feeling undecided and unsure about my future as I drove back to Pittsburgh, so when I saw the invitation in my planner, I thought, *What the heck, why not see what this is about?*

What happened was that three men from Atlanta, Georgia changed my life. David Gaylor, Gary Reed, and Rodney Harris had taken to the road with their message because they believed so strongly that the job of an advisor was to help people protect their money. Their message resonated with me because of what I had just gone through at the brokerage firm. I didn't want to have anything to do with those slimy, cookie-cutter phrases designed to manage people's emotions while they were losing their hard-earned savings.

These three men talked to us that night about the importance of protection strategies. They reiterated what I had just learned: **"You can't afford big losses when you don't have time to recover."** And they taught me about a retirement planning vehicle that gave people a *true* buffer account against market risk, one that didn't go down when the market tanked. I had no idea that you could get people into such an account—I was like, *What?*

This exists? There is a way you can get market-linked returns without losing any principal?!? I thought, *Why in the world isn't everybody doing this?!?!?*

From that day forward, I knew the fundamentals on which I would build my firm, Secure Money Advisors. And starting in 2007, that's exactly what I did. I taught people how to get a portion of their money protected in one of these buffer accounts, and if they needed to generate an income with this money, I showed them how to do that, too. Not an income dependent on market gains, but one they could count on every month. I was so energized to share this news with everybody, to tell people, "Hey, you don't have to stay in the market and lose all this money!" Business was picking up, I was feeling good about my new practice, but then guess what happened?

2008.

To this day, those clients think I'm a superhero. They think the world of me because they had these buffer accounts with me at a time when everybody else was getting wiped out. Not one of my clients who had those buffer accounts lost money that year, or any year.

I would not be where I am now without those three mentors who taught me best practices. When I realized that you didn't have to gamble with people's retirement money to get them what they needed, everything changed. Not one person at the brokerage firm where I worked said a peep about these accounts. If there ever was a word said about them, it was along the lines of, "Those are terrible accounts. You can never get your money out of them." And that turned out to be untrue. These accounts do give you liquidity options. But getting into one kind of solution alone isn't enough during today's elongated retirement. To get on the right track—and stay there—you need a totally different type of plan.

Investment Plan vs. Retirement Plan

Even when we were coming out of one of the strongest bull markets in history, the people who came to see me still didn't feel confident about having enough money for retirement. I can't tell you the number of investors who would see me after meeting with their advisor so they could get a second opinion. "Brian," they told me, "I still don't know if I can retire. I don't see any thing in writing, nothing in black and white that shows me I'll have enough income and I'll be fine."

If this is you, you're not alone. Nearly 80 percent of savers do not know what strategies exist and what options are best for securing a retirement income.[2] **The 2019 World Economic Forum reports that the average 65-year-old American could outlive their retirement savings within nine years.**[3] If this worries you, then you're probably relying on a 401(k) or some other type of investment account instead of a pension plan. What's scary about all these accounts? They invest in risk.

And yet, you need some kind of return to survive today's longer retirement. How else are you going to afford the rising cost of healthcare? How else are you going to stay relevant with inflation doubling the price of things every 20 years? But how do you balance the risk of running out against the risk of stock market loss?

What I've learned is that it's not a question of if the market comes back; it's a question of *when*. The last 100 years of returns shows us that if you can put your money in the stock market and leave it alone without touching it, then the average return will yield you around 10 percent.[4] Problem is, when you go to retire, that's when you need this money, and that's when loss suddenly matters. From 1928 until 2020, we've had a down market 27 times, or about once every 3.4 years.[5] You can't predict this stuff! Even if you average a respectable return, if you lose money at the wrong time during retirement, you can still run out of

---

2 Certified Financial Planner Board of Standards Consult Survey, New Research Confirms Americans Are Not Prepared for Retirement, May 2019, https://www.cfp.net/news/2019/05/new-research-confirms-americans-are-not-prepared-for-retirement. Accessed 11/12/2021.
3 Wood, Johnny, Retirees will outlive their savings by a decade, World Economic Forum, June 2019. https://www.weforum.org/agenda/2019/06/retirees-will-outlive-their-savings-by-a-decade/. Accessed 6/16/2021.
4 Yardeni, Edward and Abbot, Joe, Stock Market Indicators: Historical Monthly & Annual Returns, Yardeni Research Inc, May 29, 2021. https://www.yardeni.com/pub/stmktreturns.pdf. Accessed 6/16/2021.
5 Ibid.

money. So please, if you get nothing else from reading this book, understand this:

People aren't running out of money because they're not earning the right returns, they're running out because they're losing money at the wrong time.

You need to be aware of your options when funding this thing called the retirement journey. This is where having a plan on the right track comes in. It's not enough to get into a diversified portfolio with a bunch of mutual funds and stocks, with the focus of growing the money into the biggest pile. It's not enough to use the investment plan that you relied on in the past—to just keep putting the money in there and hope for the best.

A retirement plan is a completely different thing. It's designed to get you through your distribution years, and it does this by providing you with a written document in black and white that shows you exactly when and how you can retire. It includes the five key areas covered in this book: income, investment efficiency, taxation, healthcare, and legacy planning. It shows you how those five areas will be handled, but more than that, it gives you the ability to generate returns so that your portfolio can take you the distance and keep you on track. It does this by employing the new technology.

Why Isn't Everybody Doing This? Part 2

For years after founding my own firm, all I did was build my clients' portfolios around a safe money strategy. This strategy gave them principal protection and guaranteed that their income was safe. My client base grew from 500 to 700 to over 1,200 individuals. But people started asking me, "Brian, you're the only one who cares about this money. You're the only one who teaches us about taxes, risk, and legacy planning. We want you to watch over this money for us and keep some of it in the market. Please, can you do that for us?"

And I couldn't because I knew what would happen. I didn't want to go back to the traditional portfolio. I'd been on that train before, and I knew where it would lead—a one-way ticket to disaster. One day the wheels would come off the rails and things would end in a crash.

But then, I learned about the new technology.

Remember the mobile phones from the 80s? Those things were like bricks, and they couldn't even take your picture. They had to charge like seven hours for just a little bit of talk time, and they couldn't even be used outside your car. Nowadays, people don't even have home phones anymore because most of us are walking around with one in our pocket. These mobile phones are a fraction of the size, weigh hardly anything, and they can be used nearly anywhere.

Market investments have seen the same kind of advances. There's this whole new machine in the investment world called algorithms. And when I discovered how to use that, I thought, *Why in the world isn't everybody doing this?!?!?!*

I wasn't born with a silver spoon in my mouth. Growing up we didn't have much. At night I would hear my parents arguing about money, and I thought, *If I could learn about this stuff, I could really help people.* And so that's what I did—I grew up and dedicated my career to understanding money. **The strategies I teach in this book can help you stay in the market while significantly reducing your risk, giving you peace of mind and security in retirement.** That's right—the only reason the money should come out of your portfolio in retirement is to go into your pocket, not to Wall Street.

And that's what this book will focus on: I want to share with you the tools and strategies you need today to keep the train on the tracks so that during retirement, you can enjoy the ride.

We have the old way of planning for retirement: work hard and get a pension.

We have the new way: work hard and get a 401(k).

As you make the transition from an investment plan to a retirement plan, I don't want you to do it using the old rules and the old technology. I want you to have access to the latest and greatest strategies and systems that can get you everything you need. And I want to explain it to you straight without all the financial-speak so that you can really hear what I'm saying.

Folks, this doesn't have to be complicated. I'm going to show you six simple steps to build an income, limit the loss, and leave your family a legacy. I'm also going to say a lot of things that probably go against what you've always heard. This is my mission: to tell it like it is. Learn how to generate an income and replace a paycheck. Learn how to keep your money invested in a way that will significantly reduce your exposure to risk. I promise that by implementing the steps outlined in this book, you will get a plan to keep more of your hard-earned money safe and growing.

Here's to getting your retirement on the right track.

~ Brian Quaranta, President of Secure Money Advisors and investment adviser representative of Foundations Investment Advisors, LLC, an SEC-registered investment adviser.

If you're ready now: I'm so confident that I can deliver on this promise, I'm offering my readers a chance to receive a complimentary, no-obligation portfolio review. Get to know us at https://www.securemoneyadvisors.com/. Schedule your complimentary, no-obligation portfolio review by calling 724- 382-1298, or email us directly at info@securemoneyadvisors, or visit https://www.securemoneyadvisors.com/contact/. We look forward to getting to know you!

CHAPTER ONE

INVESTMENT PLAN VS. RETIREMENT PLAN WHICH DO YOU NEED?

"I hit big or miss big."

~ Babe Ruth

In the fall of 1983, a squishy-faced doll became all the rage.

Maybe you remember the Cabbage Patch Kids—they came with adoption papers and people went crazy for them. These dolls were so popular that during the holiday season, a series of violent customer outbursts that included shoving and trampling occurred at several retail stores across the United States. One of the stores that carried the dolls was the New Jersey Montgomery Ward catalog store where my dad worked.

For those of you too young to remember, catalog stores like JCPenney and Montgomery Ward were the Amazon of yesterday before you could order things online. Customers received these giant catalogs in the mail the size of phone books. Kids and grownups alike would turn the pages dreamily and circle what they wanted. Then they would come into the catalog store, speak to someone like my dad, and order the item. My dad would place the order, then make the phone call to tell the customer, "Your order has arrived. Come on in and pick it up."

During the early 80s when demand was high and Cabbage Patch Kids couldn't be ordered fast enough, employees like my dad had a real sense of job security. They were working at one of the oldest privately-held department store chains in the nation, and business was booming. No one saw it coming when, just two years later in 1985, the Montgomery Ward catalog stores folded, and my dad lost his job.

Several years later, I remember driving through Michigan in the 90s and being surprised to see one of their retail stores still standing. I thought they had all closed in 1985. Owned by General Electric and once known as the greatest retail store in America, Montgomery Ward employed approximately 32,000 people at its 250 stores nationwide. They would all eventually be shuttered in December of 2000 when they filed for Chapter 11 bankruptcy, and tens of thousands more people lost their jobs.

My dad never saw any of this coming. He went to bed one night knowing that everything was fine and woke up the next morning to discover everything in ruin. He had three kids to support, with no job and no health insurance. My parents struggled a lot after that. Dad worked two or three different jobs just to make ends meet, and while he always had a good attitude—he believed that with hard work, you could get yourself out of anything—that was the catalyst that got me thinking about money.

I saw how we went from things being okay and having enough to my dad working three jobs just so he could keep food on the table. And I thought, *There must be a way to prevent this kind of situation*. After working hard and doing so well, there's no reason a person should be financially struggling. For this reason, I dedicated my life to understanding how money works, how it accumulates, and how to protect it.

Investment plans focus purely on making the money. If you're someone like my dad who is working hard and saving for retirement, then you've probably got an investment plan. Whether the plan is through your employer in some kind of 401(k), or one you set up yourself or with a broker in an IRA, these plans are focused on one thing: earning returns. They have nothing to do with determining how much income you'll need come retirement if you lose your job, if the market falls, if your spouse dies. They can't help you if you want to leave a legacy. They don't help you figure out when and how to file for Social Security, and they certainly don't teach you how to reduce the taxes you'll have to pay. Addressing all of that requires a different kind of plan.

To grow the money, an investment plan does just fine. But to take the money out you need to go where you've never gone before, and this is what so many people get so wrong. If you want to retire, you need to get out of your investment plan and into a **retirement plan.**

"But wait a minute, Brian," I can hear you say. "I've already got myself a retirement plan. It's called a 401(k) (or a 403(b) or 457(b))." What I call those plans is a grand experiment.

> *Fast Fact: Half of all men and six out of every 10 women do not expect their income to last their lifetime.*[1]

The Grand Experiment

Back when my grandfather retired, he got a pension after working a lifetime for one employer. This pension replaced about half of his income, and that combined with his Social Security benefit and his savings gave him a good retirement. He didn't have to invest any of his money in the stock market because bank CDs back then were paying out between 10 and 15 percent, and they were FDIC-insured. He got all his income needs met from guaranteed sources with zero **risk** and his retirement was secured.

That was his plan, and it worked.

Today, more than half of the people who come into my office are retiring without a pension. They've worked for multiple employers doing different jobs and all their savings are self-directed. When companies began phasing out pensions and

---

[1] Alliance for Lifetime Income. Protected Lifetime Income Index Study – Wave 2. June 2019. https://www.protectedincome.org/wp-content/uploads/2021/03/Alliance-Protected-Lifetime-Income-Study.pdf. Accessed 5/25/2021.

replacing them with 401(k)s, 403(b)s, and 457 accounts, no one really knew how to do this.

I like to call these self-directed retirement plans "the grand experiment" because you have no idea how much these accounts will be worth when you go to take the money out. I also refer to these accounts as YO-YOs because not only do they go up and down, but You're On Your Own—LOL. Although there's really nothing funny about it. When you go to retire, what will be going on in the world? Will there be an oil crisis, a trade war, a pandemic? How will that affect the value of your investment accounts?

In other words, today you are taking a risk with something that used to be guaranteed.

A retirement benefit that used to give you a guaranteed income is now subject to the roller coaster of the stock market. And guess who's in charge of making all the decisions about how to manage this money? You!

All we want to do when we retire is to keep things the same. You want to keep the income coming in the way that you're used to and you don't want to have to worry about it. So how do you use your 401(k) or IRA or brokerage accounts to replace the paycheck that used to be provided by a pension? Let's approach this in the easiest, most stress-free way that we can.

What Kind of Retiree Are You?

There are two kinds of retirees: those who need the income and those who do not.

If you don't have a pension that you can count on from your job, then you're the kind of retiree who needs the income. So, you're going to have to ask yourself some questions.

- *Where are you going to get the income?*
- *How much income do you need?*
- *When do you need this income to start?*

If you're looking at your 401(k) or IRA, then you're looking at a bunch of investments and you're wondering what to do with them. If you're working with an advisor, he or she might have suggestions for you. They might start pulling out so many different kinds of things, you forget that income is why you're there. It's like going into a Super Walmart when all you need is toothpaste, and you start looking at everything else in the aisles—*oooh, how about this? How about that?*—and after an hour you forget what you went in there for!

If you're the kind of retiree who won't be getting a pension, and you just want to know what to do, then I've got answers for you.

If you're the other kind of retiree who does not need the income, then that means you have some kind of a pension situation that, combined with your Social Security, gives you enough income. Your problem is going to be different, but you're still going to have a problem.

It's like this: The money you have invested in your IRA or 401(k) is going to keep growing if you don't take it out for income. When the IRS says you must take it out at the age of 72, you'll be forced to do that, and to pay the taxes you owe on this money. This will affect your income taxes, your Social Security taxes, it can even affect how much you have to pay for Medicare. In other words, you're not going to be prepared for how much of this money you'll be forced to take out and pay taxes on. Your biggest problem will be Uncle Sam because without proper planning, he's likely to become the biggest beneficiary of your hard-earned retirement savings.

If you want to leave this money to your kids, then they will be forced to pay your taxes. It never really hit me how bad this situation could be until I read an article about a kid whose father had died and left him a $500,000 IRA. Now, this kid didn't know anything about IRAs or how to move this money. He was told to send in the death certificate to the company investing the money because he was the primary **beneficiary**. When he did that, the company did what they said they would do and sent him a check. Well, this young man was happy to receive the check, but he was also earning his own income. That year, he paid a tax bill of $270,000. Over half of his father's IRA—wiped out from taxation.

I ask you, how long did it take his father to build up that IRA to $270,000? How many things did he sacrifice or put off doing or go without so he could put away that money? How did he intend for his son to use this money?

I can guarantee you he did not intend for the IRS to take half of it away with one clean sweep.

Unless you want the main benefactor of your money to be Uncle Sam, then you're going to need a better way. I am writing this book to show you that better way. Whether you're the kind of retiree who needs the income or doesn't need the income, there is something you need to get before you retire. It's simple, it's not complicated, and anyone can get one.

What you need is a retirement plan.

Fast Fact: According to the 2018 Employee Benefit Research Institute report, only half of the workers surveyed said they were confident about how to withdraw income from their savings and investments.[2]

Just Stick to the Fundamentals

While I never got to see him play, my favorite baseball player growing up was Babe Ruth. My grandpa used to tell me stories about this man, known in the media as the King of Swing, the Sultan of Swat, and the Bambino, although he was born as George Herman Ruth Jr. He was a legend who hit a whopping 714 home runs and was one of only three players to hit more than 700 homers during their career.[3]

In the game of baseball, players who are known for hitting 47 to 48 home runs a season are said to be swinging for the fences.

---

2 Greenwald, Lisa; Fronstin, Paul, The State of Employee Benefits: Findings From 2018, Health and Workplace Benefits Survey, EBRI, Jan 2019 https://www.ebri.org/content/the-state-of-employee-benefits-findings-from-the-2018-health-and-workplace-benefits-survey Accessed 11/15/2021.
3 Babe Ruth Career Statistics, Family of Babe Ruth and Babe Ruth League c/o Luminary Group LLC., 2021, http://www.baberuth.com/stats/ Accessed 11/15/2021.

Their goal when they step up to the plate is to knock that ball out of the park, and so they are swinging as hard as they can. Most people know that Babe Ruth led the league for his number of home runs, but what most people don't realize is that he was also an all-time career leader in major league strikeouts.

In addition to his 714 home runs, Babe hit 1,330 strikeouts during his career.[4] In 1927, when he hit his all-time high for 60 home runs within a single season, he also had 81 strikeouts. When Babe Ruth stepped up to the plate, beloved as he was, he was actually more likely to strike out than slam it sailing over the fence. This wasn't a surprise to Babe Ruth himself, who when asked how to hit a home run replied, "I hit big or I miss big."

Most of us regular folks tend to forget this. We tend to forget that swinging for the fences is more likely to end in disappointment rather than success.

In study after study, when people who are retiring are asked, their number one fear is running out of money. Some people are even more afraid of running out than they are of death. You know intuitively that you cannot afford to lose the money that took you 35 to 40 years to save. And yet you're being told by advisors to stay in the market, to keep metaphorically swinging for the fences. Here you are with bases loaded, more money in your accounts than you've ever had in your life, and yet you keep swinging for the fences when the odds say you're most likely to strike out!

And so I ask you, "Why keep swinging for the fences when you've already won?"

An investment plan is what gets you to retirement. A retirement plan is what gets you through it.

A retirement plan doesn't have to be fancy or complicated. In fact, the ones I set up the most stick to the fundamentals of sound investing practices. They cover five basic areas: income, investment efficiency, taxes, healthcare, and **legacy planning**. Believe it or not, you can accomplish this simply, easily, and

---

[4] Baseball Almanac, updated 2021. http://www.baseball-almanac.com/hitting/histrk1.shtml. Accessed 4/2/2021.

without a lot of fuss. This is the kind of plan I got for my parents, because with a good plan in place, they were able to retire. (They also work with a good advisor, who happens to be their son.) This is the same kind of plan I want for you.

What follows are the fundamentals of a true retirement plan.

Income

If you are the kind of retiree who knows that they need their investments to produce an income, there are **safe money** solutions available. These solutions, which we will talk about in Chapter 4, can get you an income. This income will not be dependent on market performance, it will not subject your money to risk, and it can be structured to last you the rest of your life, no matter how long you live. These solutions can be had *without* fees, *without* income riders, and *without* investment sales charges. You can also list beneficiaries so that if something happens to you before all the money in the account is gone, the rest of it will go to your family, **probate**-free. You can also include an income continuation plan for your spouse.

Fast Fact: Women aged 80 and older had the highest poverty rate among all elderly persons in all age groups.[5]

Investment Efficiency

A retirement plan looks at your investments in terms of what kind of interest rate you need to generate the income that you require. If your income needs can be met with investments earning a 3 to 4 percent rate of return, then why would you keep that money in high-risk investments? Even if you need a 5 to 6 percent return, we can still get that using conservative investment strategies—meaning we can hit singles and doubles and still bring the runners in.

If you do need to keep earning double-digit returns to make the money last, we have a two-bucket strategy that we will talk about

---

[5] Congressional Research Service, Poverty Among Americans Aged 65 and Older, July 2019. CRS Report, Prepared for Members and Committees of Congress. https://fas.org/sgp/crs/misc/R45791.pdf. Accessed 3/26/2021.

in Chapter 3 that can allow you to stay in the market while getting your income as high as you can, as safely as you can, without the risk of running out of money. As I said in the introduction, this is a strategy that can give you peace of mind and security in retirement while exposing you to significantly less risk.

Legacy Planning

For those of you who are married, you have to think about what the income looks like if one of you kicks the bucket. Social Security replaces about 40 percent of earnings for the average worker.[6] It's a benefit that pays out an income for one individual's lifetime. When a household loses someone, they also lose at least one check, maybe two if that person has a pension. How are you going to replace that?

Legacy planning must also answer the IRA question. If you are the kind of retiree who doesn't need the income, how are you going to manage this money so most of it doesn't go to Uncle Sam? How can you best structure this account so that your family gets to keep the most?

Taxes

During retirement, you need to understand the impact of withdrawals when you go to spend this money. Even if you don't want to spend this money, the IRS says you have to once you hit the age of 72. What's going to happen to your income when you're forced to take out another $30,000 a year? Crossing over the threshold into a new marginal tax rate can increase your tax rate by as much as 84 percent under current law, or 67 percent using 2017 tax brackets—which we will revert to unless laws change come January of 2026. Take a look at the following visual.

---

[6] Center on Budget and Policy Priorities, Policy Basics: Top Ten Facts about Social Security, August 2020. https://www.cbpp.org/research/social-security/policy-basics-top-ten-facts-about-social-security. Accessed 10/14/2020.

Married Filing Jointly

	Old Law		Tax Cuts and Jobs Act	
10%	$0-$19,050	10%	$0-$19,050	
15%	$19,050-$77,400	12%	$19,050-$77,400	
25%	$77,400-$156,150	22%	$77,400-$165,000	
28%	$156,150-$237,950	24%	$165,000-$315,000	
33%	$237,950-$424,950	32%	$315,000-$400,000	
35%	$424,950-$480,050	35%	$400,000-$600,000	

67% Increase (brackets 15%→12%, 25%→22%)
84% Increase (brackets 22%, 24%)

Source: Urban-Brookings Tax Policy Center. Recent History of the Tax Code, "How did the Tax Cuts and Jobs Act change personal taxes?"

The goal from day one was to accumulate enough money to retire. I'm here to help you recognize that you've reached the finish line. It's the bottom of the ninth, bases are loaded, and you don't want to strike out if it could mean game over. In other words, if you've already won the game, why keep playing? Get your money out of investment plans and into a retirement plan with these five fundamentals so that it's structured to do what you need it to do.

Coming up next: I will show you why the old way of retirement planning doesn't work anymore and the danger you expose yourself to if you continue doing what you've always done.

Uncommon Answers to Common Questions

Q&A Chapter 1

After 21 years of giving live presentations on retirement planning, I know enough about these topics to have an intelligent conversation involving pretty much any question you could possibly ask. So that's why a few years ago, I ditched the canned presentation and started talking to people straight. "I want to know why you're here. What brought you in? What questions are on your mind?" I wanted to make sure that when people left my workshop, they left with real information and were glad they came.

One thing I learned this way is that the people who came to my talks were an educated group. They asked really good questions! Given that you were curious enough to pick up this book, I'm betting the same thing is true of you. Because I want you to receive real information, at the end of each chapter, I will share with you the most common questions I've heard over the years along with my uncommon answer. As always, I want you to know that as my reader, you are free to come in and talk to me about your questions any time. But even if you don't come in to see me, I want you to hear an opinion that might be different from what you've always been told.

Q: When should I file for Social Security? *I'm 62 and have to retire because my company is downsizing. I'm really okay with retiring early, but everyone keeps telling me I should wait until age 70 before I file for Social Security. Do I have to wait? If I do wait, where am I supposed to get the additional income?*

A: All Social Security claiming strategies are total bullshit. I'll give you three reasons why.

First, if you're not getting the income from Social Security, then you'll have to take it from your savings. Why spend down your own money when you can collect something guaranteed and only available to you while you're still living? Nobody can inherit your Social Security benefit. They can inherit your IRA. Why not make a plan to better structure a heritable asset?

Second, if you wait to file, that means from age 62 to age 70, you're taking that money from your retirement accounts. That's eight years of additional withdrawals. Think about the massive amount of pressure you'll have to put on those accounts in order to compensate for this. Every dollar of income you receive from Social Security is one dollar less your retirement account has to earn.

And third, most people when they retire want to start doing all the things they promised themselves they would do. If you want to go on vacation or just travel, or if a house emergency comes up, you want to have the money for that. At the beginning of retirement, there's a 10-to-15-year window when people want as much money as they can to get out there and do those big bucket-list things. Filing early for your Social Security might be the only way you can get that.

Now, of course everyone's situation is different. Waiting to file does significantly increase your benefit. The time of your filing should make sense for your lifestyle, your health, your spouse if you're married, and the current assets that you have. In my experience, advisors want to sound like they're so smart by telling you they can optimize Social Security, but in the grand scheme of things, what can extend the life of your portfolio even more is an advisor who can give you a true retirement plan.

CHAPTER TWO

THINK LIKE A PENSIONER, NOT A GAMBLER

WILL YOU HAVE ENOUGH TO STAY RETIRED?

"It ain't over till it's over."

~ *Yogi Berra*

Picture this: You're sitting around the dinner table during Thanksgiving, getting caught up with family members you haven't seen in a while. Your belly is full of turkey and stuffing and the football game is playing in the background. A commercial comes on for an investment firm and the conversation turns to money. The stock market has been wobbly lately. You mention that you're thinking of getting out of the market and going into something safer because you're getting closer to retirement. And suddenly everyone in the room has an opinion about what you should do.

"Ah, no, you don't want to do that," the person next to you says. "You'll never earn anything if you get out of the market."

"Have you seen the kind of interest rates banks are paying?"

"Yeah, it's like nothing."

"But I need this money for my retirement income," you say. "I can't afford to lose it."

"It's only a paper loss until you sell," someone says.

It never feels like a paper loss, you think.

"Just keep the money invested and live off 4 percent."

Does that strategy still work? you wonder.

"Remember, you're in it for the long haul."

Where have you heard that before?

These are the things that people say about money when the money is not theirs to lose. But who are you to question conventional wisdom? Who are you to argue with people you respect? If the market works for them then why go against the grain? Why try to reinvent the wheel? You've heard about the 4 percent rule, and it's worked for a few of your friends.

Still, there's that nagging feeling that won't go away.

I find it very interesting that most people know deep inside what they want to do with their money. I can't tell you the number of times I've had people say to me, "That's what I think, too!" But when they talk to their advisor, he or she has an answer for every question and a pie chart for every concern. It might be advice that goes against your gut, but it echoes what everybody else is saying, and so you leave their office more confused. You go home feeling nervous and uncertain and worried that your plan will fail. You hold your breath every time the stock market drops, and you're afraid to do what you really want with this money because you're afraid it will run out.

This isn't the way it has to be. Even if you won't be receiving a pension from your employer, there is a way you can structure your portfolio to give you a regular income that doesn't feel like gambling. It's easy to see the comparisons between the stock market and the casino. We feel good going in, but unless we keep the alcohol flowing, we probably won't feel so good coming out. You play the best hand you can, but at the end of the day, a gambler has no control over the outcome, and just like being in the stock market, there's never any guarantee of a win.

A pensioner, on the other hand, is set up to receive a guaranteed payment every month during retirement. That payment will continue to arrive, regardless of stock market performance or how long they live. There's no guesswork to it, no selling and buying, no worry or stress. The pensioner knows their income is coming and so they are free to enjoy their retirement without the fear that it will fail.

If you're building a retirement plan so that you're in a position where it might fail, then you're not planning—you're gambling. Yes, there is a way to stay invested in the market without feeling like you're betting the family farm. Yes, it is possible to keep up with **inflation** and secure an income. And you don't have to stay in the market unless you want to. In this chapter, I'm going to show you why all the things that people say about what to do with this money are no longer true.

Let's start with an oldy but goody: the 4 percent rule.

Fast Fact: In today's low-interest-rate world, investors who stick with traditionally-allocated portfolios and withdraw 4 percent for income have a failure rate of 57 percent.[7]

The Old Technology

When I was growing up, we had just one phone. It was the family phone and it hung on the wall in the hallway between the kitchen and the bathroom in its yellow cradle with a long curly cord. It never did reach into my bedroom, so I had to sit in the hall closet if I wanted privacy to talk to my girlfriend. Of course, everyone knew when I was in the closet talking to my girlfriend because that cord would be stretched across the hall where it disappeared behind the door. Even if I locked the door, my brother could listen in, or my dad might pound on the door, "Brian, I need to use the phone!" Or my mom would ask me some mortally embarrassing question like, "Honey, could you set the table for dinner, please?"

[7] Finke, Michael, Pfau, Wade, Blanchett, David, The 4 Percent Rule is Not Safe in a Low-Yield World, The Journal of Financial Planning, 2013 https://www.onefpa.org/journal/Pages/The%204%20Percent%20 Rule%20Is%20Not%20Safe%20in%20a%20Low-Yield%20World.aspx Accessed 11/15/2021.

Back in the old days, we didn't have personal cell phones with which to have private conversations. Not even my parents still have their old wall phone—they got a cordless model one year for Christmas. This to say, when better technology comes along that solves the problems inherent in the old way of doing things, most people learn to embrace it.

But sometimes old habits die hard. New technology can be unfamiliar if you don't have the right equipment or understand how to use it. The 4 percent rule is like that old wall phone: It's simple to use and easy to understand, albeit problematic and outdated. Designed by a financial planner named William Bengen in the 1990s, 4 percent is the amount of money, adjusted annually for inflation, that retirees are supposedly able to withdraw from their market accounts without the risk of failure. When William Bengen did the math using historical stock market returns, he found that withdrawing 4 percent annually had a low failure rate of 6 percent.

But he was using numbers from a completely different century.

Today, we are in a low-interest-rate environment with a global market that can rise or fall based on a tweet. A record number of people are retiring, which means more money is moving out of the market even more rapidly, causing even more **volatility**. We are also living longer, which puts even more pressure on your portfolio.

Experts now find the projected failure rate for retirement accounts following the 4 percent withdrawal rule has jumped to 57 percent.[8]

Are you willing to accept these odds?

Let's take a look at why this happens.

If you're taking money out every month and the market goes down, not only are you locking in the loss, you're compounding it. Most people underestimate what kind of return they'll need

---
8 Ibid.

just to get back to even. The **math of rebounds** doesn't work the way you think it should. Think you need a 50 percent gain to recover after a 50 percent loss? Think again. What you need is a 100 percent return instead. The following visual shows you why.

Source: Magellan Financial.

To counter this, I've seen people go into conservative mode with bond-heavy portfolios, thinking this **diversification** will give them a buffer against risk. What happens instead is these portfolios underperform during good markets and perform very badly during bad markets. During 2008 I saw portfolios with these types of allocations lose by as much as 25 percent, and they didn't reap the gains afterward to recover from the loss. If you're taking a 25 percent loss on top of your 4 percent withdrawal, and not earning competitive returns, you can see how very quickly that could cause your portfolio to fail.

One obvious solution to the 4 percent rule is to lower the income amount by withdrawing closer to 2 percent. Most people need more income than that. And after saving a lifetime for retirement, the last thing you want to do is be tight with this money, too afraid to do all the things you've always wanted to do. You deserve a better strategy than that.

Fast Fact: *The 4% rule for income withdrawal has now shriveled to only 2.4% for investors taking a moderate amount of risk in today's post-pandemic world.*[9]

The Retirement Red Zone

Bill and his sister Jill were three years apart. They both retired early at the age of 62, and they both retired with a $1 million portfolio. Their portfolios each earned the same rate of return—just over 8 percent annually. They also both followed the 4 percent rule, withdrawing $40,000 for their income during year one, and then increasing that to allow for inflation every year afterward. The only thing they did differently was retire at different times.

Bill retired in 1996, and his portfolio for the first three years after retirement experienced robust returns. He endured the Lost Decade that started in 2000 when his portfolio saw three years of negative returns, followed by a 38 percent loss in 2008. But he stayed in the market and continued to withdraw his income. In 2019, at the age of 85, Bill had a nice cushy account balance of just over $2 million. He was not in danger of running out. Take a look at the chart.

---

[9] Rusoff, Jane Wollman, "Wade Pfau: Pandemic Tears Up 4% Rule," Think Advisor, April 2020, https://www.thinkadvisor.com/2020/04/14/wade-pfau-virus-crisis-has-slashed-4-rule-nearly-in-half/ Accessed 11/15/2021.

The Impact of Sequence Risk
Bill Jones:
Age at Retirement: 62

Growth Bucket (S&P Index)

Year	Initial Premium/ Beginning Balance	Growth Percentage	Growth Amount	Withdrawl	End of Year
1996	$1,000,000.00	20.26%	$202,600.00	$(40,000.00)	$1,162,600.00
1997	$1,162,600.00	31.01%	$360,522.26	$(41,200.00)	$1,481,922.26
1998	$1,481,922.26	26.67%	$395,228.67	$(42,436.00)	$1,834,714.93
1999	$1,834,714.93	19.53%	$358,319.83	$(43,709.08)	$2,149,325.68
2000	$2,149,325.68	-10.14%	($217,941.62)	$(45,020.35)	$1,886,363.71
2001	$1,886,363.71	-13.04%	($245,981.83)	$(46,370.96)	$1,594,010.91
2002	$1,594,010.91	-23.37%	($372,520.35)	$(47,762.09)	$1,173,728.47
2003	$1,173,728.47	26.38%	$309,629.57	$(49,194.95)	$1,434,163.09
2004	$1,434,163.09	8.99%	$128,931.26	$(50,670.80)	$1,512,423.54
2005	$1,512,423.54	3.00%	$45,372.71	$(52,190.93)	$1,505,605.33
2006	$1,505,605.33	13.62%	$205,063.45	$(53,756.66)	$1,656,912.12
2007	$1,656,912.12	3.53%	$58,489.00	$(55,369.35)	$1,660,031.77
2008	$1,660,031.77	-38.49%	($638,946.23)	$(57,030.44)	$964,055.10
2009	$964,055.10	23.45%	$226,070.92	$(58,741.35)	$1,131,384.67
2010	$1,131,384.67	12.78%	$144,590.96	$(60,503.59)	$1,215,472.04
2011	$1,215,472.04	0.00%	$0.00	$(62,318.70)	$1,153,153.35
2012	$1,153,153.35	13.41%	$154,637.86	$(64,188.26)	$1,243,602.95
2013	$1,243,602.95	29.60%	$368,106.47	$(66,113.91)	$1,545,595.52
2014	$1,545,595.52	11.39	$176,043.33	$(68,097.32)	$1,653,541.52
2015	$1,653,541.52	-0.73%	($12,070.85)	$(70,140.24)	$1,571,330.43
2016	$1,571,330.43	9.54%	$149,904.92	$(72,244.45)	$1,648,990.90
2017	$1,648,990.90	19.42%	$320,234.03	$(74,411.78)	$1,894,813.15
2018	$1,894,813.15	-6.24%	($118,236.34)	$(76,644.14)	$1,699,932.67
2019	$1,699,932.67	28.88%	$490,940.56	$(78,943.46)	$2,111,929.77
	Total Account Value:		$ 2,111,929.77		

Source: Author's own calculations.[10]

His sister Jill, on the other hand, retired in 1999. Instead of three good years in the market after retirement, she experienced three bad years at the very start of the Lost Decade. That on top of her withdrawals of 4 percent crippled her portfolio. Even though she stayed in the market and earned the same returns as her brother, her portfolio was never able to recover. In 2019, at the age of 82, Jill has many more years left to live—women tend to live longer

---

[10] The information used in this historical S&P 500 chart was extracted from Yahoo.com/finance over a 24-year period and is not a guarantee of future results or performance. Illustration does not include taxes and fees and is not representative of an actual product or indicative of market performance.

than men and she's already three years younger than her brother. And yet her account balance has shriveled to $148,000. That's enough to give her two more years of income, and that's it.

Jill is facing every retiree's nightmare: *running out of money before running out of life.*

The Impact of Sequence Risk
Jill Jones:
Age at Retirement: 62

Growth Bucket (S&P Index)

Year	Initial Premium/ Beginning Balance	Growth Percentage	Growth Amount	Withdrawl	End of Year
1999	$1,000,000.00	19.53%	$195,300.00	$(40,000.00)	$1,155,300.00
2000	$1,155,300.00	-10.14%	($117,147.42)	$(41,200.00)	$996,952.58
2001	$996,952.58	-13.04%	($130,002.62)	$(42,436.00)	$824,513.96
2002	$824,513.96	-23.37%	($192,688.91)	$43,709.08)	$588,115.97
2003	$588,115.97	26.38%	$155,144.99	$(45,020.35)	$698,240.61
2004	$698,240.61	8.99%	$62,771.83	$(46,370.96)	$714,641.47
2005	$714,641.47	3.00%	$21,439.24	$(47,762.09)	$688,318.62
2006	$688,318.62	13.62%	$93,749.00	$(49,194.95)	$732,872.67
2007	$732,872.67	3.53%	$25,870.41	$(50,670.80)	$708,072.27
2008	$708,072.27	-38.49%	($272,537.02)	$(52,190.93)	$383,344.33
2009	$383,344.33	23.45%	$89,894.24	$(53,756.66)	$419,481.91
2010	$419,481.91	12.78%	$53,609.79	$(55,369.35)	$417,722.35
2011	$417,722.35	0.00%	$0.00	$(57,030.44)	$360,691.91
2012	$360,691.91	13.41%	$48,368.79	$(58,741.35)	$350,319.35
2013	$350,319.35	29.60%	$103,694.53	$(60,503.59)	$393,510.29
2014	$393,510.29	11.39%	$44,820.82	$(62,318.70)	$376,012.42
2015	$376,012.42	-0.73%	($2,744.89)	$(64,188.26)	$309,079.27
2016	$309,079.27	9.54%	$29,486.16	$(66,113.91)	$272,451.53
2017	$272,451.53	19.42%	$52,910.09	$(68,097.32)	$257,264.29
2018	$257,264.29	-6.24%	($16,053.29)	$(70,140.24)	$171,070.76
2019	$171,070.76	28.88%	$49,405.24	$(72,244.45)	$148,231.55

Total Account Value: $ 148,231.55

Source: Author's own calculations.[11]

---

[11] The information used in this historical S&P 500 chart was extracted from Yahoo.com/finance over a 24-year period and is not a guarantee of future results or performance. Illustration does not include taxes and fees and is not representative of an actual product or indicative of market performance.

Fast Fact: Women live on average five years longer than men.[12]

What did Jill do that was so wrong? She saved the same amount of money as her brother, she invested the same way, and she averaged the same return. What happened to Jill was a timing mistake that was absolutely out of her control. It's a phenomenon known by financial planners as **sequence risk.**

Sequence risk is a risk created by the order or sequence of market returns once withdrawals are coming out of the portfolio.

This risk is something you have no control over. You can't predict what the market will do during the years just after you retire. What's more, this risk can also impact the retiree who is inside what I call the *retirement red zone*. This is a danger zone I define as the years just before and after your time of retirement when your assets are most vulnerable to sequence risk. Allow me to explain by indulging in another sporting metaphor.

In the game of football, the area 20 yards in from the goal line is known as the red zone. When you're playing inside this red zone, not only are you getting closer to scoring big, you're also running out of time and space. The field is getting smaller, your opponent is bearing down, and the pressure is on you to win. The last thing in the world you want to do is fumble the ball.

This is exactly the kind of pressure on your portfolio once it gets closer to the retirement line, and it's why I advocate for changing your strategy. You want to move from an investment plan into a retirement plan so your portfolio can stay nimble and maintain the big returns you've already earned. Why in the world would you risk throwing a Hail Mary pass now when the other team could intercept, steal the ball, and run it to the other end of the field for a touchdown?

Maybe it's not your style to take a knee and run out the clock—I understand. Maybe you love the heat and excitement of the game.

---

12 Kockanek, Kenneth D.; Jiaquan, Xu; Arias, Elizabeth, Mortality in the United States, 2019. National Center for Health Statistics, Centers for Disease Control and Prevention, December 2020. https://www.cdc.gov/nchs/products/databriefs/db395.htm. Accessed 4/07/2021.

You don't have to get out of the market just because you retire. There are strategies I'll share with you in this book that allow you to stay in the game without the risk of losing it all. But first, if you're the type of retiree who needs the income, then you have to look at how you're going to allocate the money you need to live on.

You want to think like a pensioner, not a gambler! This has to be your number one priority because what the research tells us is what I see happening to the people who come into my office every day: People aren't running out of money because they're earning the wrong return, they are running out because they're retiring at the wrong time.

Don't let sequence risk prevent you from living the kind of retirement you've worked so hard to earn. The old way of generating income from market investments is no longer safe during today's times. The old technology is broke, but you don't have to be!

Stay with me and keep turning the page. Up next, I will share with you the two-bucket approach that can help you generate income or grow a legacy with an investment strategy that exposes your money to significantly less risk.

Uncommon Answers to Common Questions

Q&A Chapter 2

Question: Should I pay off the house? *Brian, I'm about four years away from retirement. My wife and I have some money saved and we own our home. It has a mortgage of $2,500 a month. What's my best strategy here? Should my wife and I take advantage of catch-up contributions for our IRA and 401(k)? Do we invest that money in something else? Or do we pay off the mortgage on the house?*

Answer: I'm sure you've been told by industry experts that keeping a mortgage is the smartest financial move. Given today's low-interest rates, you stand to gain more in market returns than what you're paying in interest, and so most advisors would tell you to keep investing without paying off the house. I disagree and here's why.

You're four years away from retirement, entering the red zone. We've just seen how the unpredictability of the market can work against you. If you invest that money in your 401(k) or a brokerage account, there's a chance you could lose it just before you retire. What investment stands to give you the greatest probability of success?

Paying off the house.

Think in terms of a pensioner and look at the income. If you pay off that mortgage, that's $2,500 you are *guaranteed* to pick up every month in addition to the income you have coming in. That's $2,500 a month that your portfolio *does not have to earn*. You'd have to contribute another $750,000 to generate $2,500 a month using the 4 percent rule. And that's assuming the market cooperates! You just don't know.

But you do know that every dollar you put toward the mortgage will go to work for you. This is not advice you'll get from a typical advisor because they want you to keep those dollars invested with them where they'll stand to earn commissions or fees.

CHAPTER THREE

LEVERAGE THE POWER OF THE TWO-BUCKET STRATEGY

"Simplicity is about subtracting the obvious and adding the meaningful."

~ John Maeda

Getting information during the age of the internet is easy, but that information is by no means simple to interpret. A 2019 survey conducted by Eligibility found that 89 percent of us google our health symptoms before going to the doctor.[13] This has led to a phenomenon that some medical experts are calling "cyberchondria." People become convinced they have cancer when what they really have is an ingrown hair. Curious, I took a look at the study and found that in my home state of Pennsylvania, the most googled symptom was stress.[14]

Rather than helping people to become better educated about their health, googling and then drawing conclusions based on incomplete information can lead you down a path of paranoia and worry, and if stress is why you're googling, then that could turn into a bad situation fast. What's also concerning is that I've noticed the same kind of trend happening in the financial industry. People are googling their financial questions in an attempt to get educated, and instead what they're getting is only more worried and confused.

13, The Most Googled Medical Symptoms by State, Eligibility MEDICARE, March 2019. https://eligibility.com/medicare/states-most-googled-medical-symptom. Accessed 4/19/2021.
14 Ibid.

I think it's great that people are curious enough to ask these questions, but getting your answers online will give you incomplete information at best. At worse, it could prevent you from taking action at a time when it's vital to act, such as the years just before and during retirement.

Conventional wisdom tells us that the way to avoid running out of money is to earn as much interest as possible. **And yet over 40 percent of all U.S. households headed by someone aged 35 to 64 are projected to run short of money during retirement.**[15] If the goal of your investments during retirement is to generate an income, then you have to ask yourself how you are going to do that. How can you get your income as high as you can, as safely as you can, without running out of money?

My solution is the two-bucket strategy. Even if you're the kind of retiree who doesn't need the income, who couldn't benefit from a strategy that can decrease your risk?

Yes, you read that correctly. In this chapter, I am going to show you how to leverage the tremendous power behind the two-bucket approach. The goal of this strategy is to achieve the highest income you can, as safely as you can, while at the same time reducing your risk. *How is this possible?!?* Think about it: you know that success in the market requires a long-term commitment where you leave this money alone. But how in the hell can you do that during retirement when it's finally time to spend it?

The answer is the two-bucket approach.

Fast Fact: Most people can assume a retirement income replacement ratio of 80 percent, meaning they'll spend about 80 percent of the income they were making before retirement.[16]

---

[15] VanDerhei, Jack, Retirement Savings Shortfalls: Evidence from EBRI's 2019 Retirement Security Projection Model, EBRI Issue Brief, March 2019. https://www.ebri.org/retirement/publications/issue-briefs/content/retirement- savings-shortfalls-evidence-from-ebri-s-2019-retirement-security-projection-model. Accessed 4/22/2021.
[16] Fidelity Viewpoints, "How Much Will You Spend in Retirement?" September 2021 https://www.fidelity.com/viewpoints/retirement/spending-in-retirement Accessed 11/15/2021.

3 Steps to an Income Plan

Every year there's a new diet fad everybody goes crazy for, some surefire-way to take off those unwanted pounds, a way to get thin and—the real test—stay thin. Remember when eggs were bad? When we were supposed to eat only bacon and cheese? Only plants?

Whether it's Atkins, Paleo, or Richard Simmons, these plans worked when they aligned with the fundamentals of eating right and getting enough exercise. If people managed to do that while they were also eating their bacon and kale, then they lost weight. But did they keep it off?

Another thing I googled was this: Of all the high-income countries in the world, the United States has the highest rates of obesity.[17] So, probably not. This is why sticking to the fundamentals is best.

My industry has also overcomplicated retirement and made basic income planning harder than it has to be. We've gotten away from the fundamentals of a sound approach when those principles can still work. The goal of any income plan is simple: to keep your lifestyle the same. During retirement, you want your income to feel the same as it did when you were working. The two-bucket strategy is a simple way you can achieve this objective.

To continue our stay-fit metaphor, one bucket is about eating right to keep you fueled, AKA, the income. The second bucket is there to keep you moving, AKA, your account growing in the right direction—which is upwards. To implement this approach, I take my clients through three simple steps.

Step 1: Identify the Need

First, I teach my clients how to mathematically figure out how much income they need to withdraw from their accounts every month. You can do that by assessing the monthly expenses you currently have. My tips here are to remember to include your

---

[17] Obesity Trends, Harvard School of Public Health, Copyright © 2021 The President and Fellows of Harvard College, https://www.hsph.harvard.edu/obesity-prevention-source/obesity-trends/. Accessed 4.19.2021.

car loans unless you'll have that paid off come retirement, and if you're retiring early, you'll have to add in healthcare. You won't qualify for Medicare until you reach age 65, so you will want to budget an amount per month for health insurance and add that to the expense column. For married couples, this might be times two.

A simple way to make sure you consider all the little expenses—things like your nephew's birthday present, your dog's haircut, and the time you picked up the breakfast tab for a friend—I have a little trick for you. Keep all your living expenses coming out from one checking account. That way, all you have to do to calculate your expense planning is add up the withdrawals and divide by 12.

We don't want to restrict you in retirement. The goal is to keep things the same. I like to be very mathematical with this step and look at the real numbers so you can continue to enjoy the lifestyle you're accustomed to.

Step 2: Get that Income Protected and Safe

We build income plans around protection because when people know they have this element secured, they don't have to feel fearful or anxious. You don't have to worry about what's going on in the stock market, and you don't have to ask Dr. Google what to do about your insomnia or stress. Low-risk investments are a great way to approach the income portion of your retirement. The trick is to employ them the minute you enter the danger zone and not after a loss has already occurred.

To help you with this timing, there is a fundamental rule known as **The Rule of 100**. This simple tool is used to determine the correct portion of risk and safety—kind of like the FDA recommendation to eat a certain number of fruits and vegetables every day. Simply subtract your age from 100 and keep your risk investments under that percentage.

THE RULE OF 100
100 – YOUR AGE = % of your portfolio in RISK

For example, a 60-year-old woman would have no more than 40 percent of her portfolio in the stock market with 60 percent protected in low-risk investments. As you reach a new decade, adjust the scale.

You might also adjust the scale depending on your risk tolerance and whether you are the kind of retiree who needs the income or not. If you know you need the income, you might not want to roll the dice with 40 percent of your portfolio. Whatever the income number you landed on in step one, you want to know that amount is coming to you in the form of guaranteed funds. Social Security is one such source of guaranteed income, but if you're like most people, then you're going to need another source. There are options available other than risk investments and in Chapter 4, I'm going to tell you about them.

Step 3: Get that Income as High as You Can

While no one is likely to argue the value of getting your income as high as possible, I'd like to point out a few key things.

First, for married couples, you always want to look at what happens to the income when one spouse dies. Social Security is an income that pays out for life, so when you lose a spouse, you also lose at least one paycheck from Social Security. What other sources of income will disappear? Because everybody's Social Security and pension income is different, you'll want to consider both scenarios: What if the wife dies? What if the husband dies? While I know it's not pleasant to think about now, it's far better to plan for this on paper before it happens in real life.

By plotting out an income spreadsheet, we can see the drop in income before it occurs so that you won't have to experience it.

Fast Fact: Women are 80% more likely than men to be impoverished in retirement.[18]

Another reason to get the income as high as possible is to plan for increasing taxation and long-term care events. At our firm, we reassess this part of the plan every year because tax laws change. It might be possible to do tax *planning* now, during your early years, so that your tax *paying* is lower during your later years. Reducing taxation is one way to increase your income because more of it is yours to keep! For some people, their expenses are higher during their early years when they are out and about, traveling and doing things. For other people, health issues come up during their later years and add significant expenses to the monthly budget. You'll want your advisor to tailor a plan that can increase your income when you need it most.

Fast Fact: Expect 15% of your living expenses to be related to healthcare expenses after you retire, not counting the cost of assisted living or long-term care.[19]

And lastly, you'll want to consider why getting the income as high as possible might also mean keeping your expenses as low as possible. Once you maximize your 401(k) contributions to take advantage of any free money from your employer, look at ways you can erase your debt load. That might include getting that mortgage paid off like we talked about at the end of Chapter 2. Getting the mortgage paid down is usually very beneficial for most people, as it will free up quite a bit of cash flow.

All these considerations are yet another reason to transition from an *investment plan* into a *retirement plan* years before you retire. Not only can you get a portion of that money protected, but your advisor can conduct an annual review. Did you lose a job, add a family member, or buy a house? As things change, we'll want to make adjustments to the cash flow model or investment

---

18 National Institute on Retirement Security, Women 80% More Likely to Be Impoverished in Retirement, March 2016. https://www.nirsonline.org/2016/03/women-80-more-likely-to-be-impoverished-in- retirement/. Accessed 4/23/2021.
19 Fidelity Viewpoints, "How Much Will You Spend in Retirement?" April 2019. https://www.fidelity.com/viewpoints/retirement/spending-in-retirement. Accessed 4/29/2021.

strategy so we're not missing anything. Retirement is anywhere from a 20-to-30-year period of time. We want to make sure that everything stays up to date. One of the ways we do that is by creating a withdrawal worksheet.

The 3 Interest Rates that Matter

It's really fun to watch the money pile up and grow; it can be totally nerve-wracking to watch it drain away. That's why we do a **withdrawal worksheet**. Using our withdrawal worksheet, we can project out how much income you'll receive every month, how much the account is projected to earn, and when or if the money will run out. When you can see how long the money will last, we can also project what kind of interest rate you need to keep the stress at bay.

I always tell my clients that plotting is the fun part. This is when we plug your numbers into the model to determine what kind of interest rate you need. We base this on the number of withdrawals required to get you to age 100. We might start out with a 6 percent rate, then lower the rate to 5 percent, 4 percent, and so on. As I bring the interest rate down, the model is recalculating itself to show us how long the account will last before it reaches zero. The goal is to see how low we can get the interest rate while still maintaining enough income.

Now, we don't always want the account to get to zero. You might have other goals with this money, such as leaving a legacy to your family. This is why I run illustration using three different interest rates. It's only when we know what the money needs to earn that we can get a target on what kind of risk we need to take. From there, we can decide how much of your portfolio should go into each of the two buckets.

For example, if you need to earn 5 percent, then I know you're not going to be able to get that rate in a guarantee. To counter that, we might allocate a higher percentage into the growth bucket than we would if earning a 3 to 4 percent return would take care of your needs. (Because why swing for the fences and put more of your money than necessary at risk? We don't want you to strike out during the pivotal moment that could mean game over for retirement.)

What follows are the three interest rates we look for when modeling a retirement plan:

1. **Spend Down Interest Rate.** This is the interest rate you need to earn to keep your account healthy for a specific period of time that, when over, would result in a zero account balance. If your plan is to spend all the money while you're alive, then you'll want to identify your spend down rate.

2. **Preservation Rate.** This is the rate you need if you want to be able to make withdrawals on the account while still preserving the **principal**. The principal is the amount of money you initially put into the account, not the growth. The goal of this rate is to spend the growth without depleting the principal, a goal that has proven more difficult given our low interest rate environment and the impact of sequence risk.

3. **Legacy Rate.** This is the rate you'll need if you want to leave some amount of money to your beneficiaries. Whether you're the kind of retiree who needs the income or who doesn't need the income, this rate will ensure that there is money left in the portfolio at the time of your death. And for the kind of retiree who doesn't need the income, this will be an important interest rate to discover. If you know you want to leave your IRA for your family, for example, then we will want to plan carefully for a legacy rate that considers the impact of the **required minimum distribution** (RMD) demanded by the IRS once you reach a certain age. Otherwise, Uncle Sam may become your biggest beneficiary.

Retirement planning is a broad-brush term—what does it really entail? In a nutshell, you want to know what the income will look like now and later. You need to know that your income picture will stay the same or look close enough when one spouse dies, and you want to keep pace with inflation, changes to tax rates, and expenses related to long-term care. And lastly, you want to understand the impact of your withdrawals. How fast or slow will this money drain away? As you're taking money out of the account, what is the interest rate doing to help you keep up? And how will you account for what I call "as need withdrawals?"

An "as need withdrawal" is not the same thing as an income withdrawal. "As need" is when an event pops up and suddenly you need the money. For instance, what happens if you take out an "as need withdrawal" of $30,000 to remodel the kitchen after the sink springs a leak? Can the account support this withdrawal and continue to grow? Or will it start to shrink? Imagine the impact of an "as need withdrawal" on top of income withdrawals to a losing account, and you'll understand why this planning exercise is so important. It will point you in the right direction of the interest rate you need to accomplish your goals of sustained growth—or the draining of your portfolio—depending on what you want.

> **Fast Fact:** Research suggests that if you plan to travel and lead an active lifestyle, then you'll need to ratchet up your overall retirement budget by 6%.[20]

How to Significantly Reduce Your Risk

Now for the moment we've all been waiting for, yes? When we know how much income you need and what rate of return is required to sustain and achieve your goals, the final task at hand is to figure out how much of your portfolio to allocate to bucket one, and how much to allocate to bucket two.

Go to any traditional financial planner with your retirement-specific concerns, and they will probably talk to you about asset allocation and the 4 percent rule. But what kind of meaningful

---

20 Fidelity Viewpoints, "How Much Will You Spend in Retirement?" April 2019. https://www.fidelity.com/viewpoints/retirement/spending-in-retirement. Accessed 4/29/2021.

asset allocation can that really do for you? We already talked about why advisors can't move you in and out of different funds—they don't want to get accused of churning, and they have to follow the SEC 35d-1 rule.

In the last chapter, we uncovered the research that exposes the fundamental problem with the 4 percent rule. Bill Bengen was working with numbers from the last century, and he never looked at the risk of receiving unfavorable returns in the wrong order, which, based on the year you retire, could drastically change your situation. Remember Bill and his sister Jill? The only thing Jill did differently than her brother was retire three years later. She saved the same $1 million and earned the same average rate of return, and yet she ran out of money. Nobody wants to be Jill.

My friend and colleague Dave Gaylor uncovered all of this when he wrote his book *Income Allocation*. He was one of the first to ever teach the strategy I'm about to share with you now, and so you might already be familiar with the basic idea behind it. But for my friend's sake, I want to give him credit. This is a two-bucket approach to asset allocation now used by thousands of retirement specialists everywhere. While it's been called a lot of different things, the goal of the approach is always the same: to keep your lifestyle intact. Once you understand mathematically how much income you need to withdraw from this pile of money, then you can roll up your sleeves to accomplish the correct balance of growth and safety.

Here is how it's done.

Bucket #1: Safe Income

First, we get the income safe. To do this, we create a buffer account where the money is protected from market loss and the principal is guaranteed. That's right—the amount you put into the first bucket is guaranteed to never go down due to market loss. This account should also offer the ability to earn enough interest to help you keep up with inflation.

I like to label this bucket as green because it allows your cash to flow. Think of it as your pension money and your buffer account against risk. If the market fell tomorrow, you wouldn't have to bite off all your nails because you would know that the money is in the green bucket where it's safe from market loss. It won't fluctuate based on the tweet of the hour, it won't be dependent on earning a certain return, and you won't have to worry about buying low or selling high. Your buffer account will either go up or stay the same based on the index until the payments start.

For example, if you have a $1 million portfolio and you need $20,000 in annual income, then you'll be able to put X amount into the green bucket to generate that $20,000 while knowing the principal is guaranteed. Your X amount is determined by your three interest rates because everyone's situation is different. But you'll want to have peace of mind knowing that your $20,000 income is guaranteed.

Many of these buffer accounts also allow you to set the income flow for life, meaning the payments will continue for as long as you live—for both you and your spouse, if that is what you want to do. Other accounts give you the option of an increasing income like the **cost-of-living adjustment** (COLA) that you get from Social Security to keep up with inflation. I will show you more about how to choose from among these different accounts in the next chapter.

Bucket #2: Growth Money

The second bucket is your growth fund. This is where you will put the money that you don't need to withdraw for an immediate income. Because you're not planning to touch this money for another 10 to 15 years, it has the ability to benefit from long-term market growth. By dividing your portfolio into two buckets, you'll be able to reap the rewards of competitive returns while at the same time reducing your risk.

In a nutshell, here's how it works:

Investor A put $1 million in the stock market and then retired, withdrawing a 4 percent income of $40,000 annually in good market conditions and bad. At the end of 20 years, he had an account balance of $433,000.[21]

Investor B used the two-bucket approach. He put $500,000 in the income bucket and $500,000 in the growth bucket. He withdrew the same $40,000 of income until the income bucket ran out, and after 20 years, the growth bucket had grown to $974,000.[22] So now, he could tap into that money and start the strategy again.

Using this strategy, the investor did 100 percent better with his money while exposing himself to significantly less risk, thus achieving a higher probability of success. Do you see how powerful this strategy can be? It protects you from being Jill. It works because of this simple fact:

Your portfolio will average a higher overall rate of return if you don't withdraw the money.

By leveraging the two-bucket approach, you can keep your retirement on the right track. Get the protection you need to keep your income the same, along with the growth required to build a legacy, plan for expense increases, or fund the travel adventures and other activities you've always envisioned doing during your retirement years.

Now that you know how the two-bucket strategy works, our next chapters will focus on the kinds of investments that can best keep your buckets full.

Uncommon Answers to Common Questions

Q&A Chapter 3

Question: How can I access the money in my 401(k) before age 59 ½? *I've been working since I could walk. For the last 35 years, I've*

---

[21] These numbers were calculated using the historical S&P 500® chart extracted from Yahoo.com/finance. These S&P results are for illustrative purposes only and should not be deemed a representation of past or future results.
[22] Ibid.

been with one company, and now I'm done and ready to retire. But I'm only 57. My pension doesn't kick in until I turn 59 ½. I can't access the money in my 401(k), either, because there's a 10 percent tax penalty if I withdraw this money before age 59 ½. Still, I need an income now. Should I roll this money into an IRA? Am I eligible for an in-service withdrawal? My friend says that I should use something called the 72T Rule and withdraw equal payments. What's the best strategy here?

Answer: There are several ways you can access the money in your 401(k) before age 59 ½ without having to pay the 10 percent penalty assessed by the IRS, but here's the catch: Not all of these strategies will protect you from sequence risk. Furthermore, you won't qualify for all of them, and they won't all be in your best interest.

You won't qualify for an in-service withdrawal because those only apply when you're still employed by the company. An easy way to remember this is that in order to qualify, you must still be in service for your employer.

The 72T Rule, known as the Substantially Equal Periodic Payment (SEPP) exemption, isn't in your best interest, either. Based on IRS section 72(t), this distribution rule states that if you want to generate income out of a retirement account before age 59 ½, then you must take the money out in equal payments every single year for five years, or until age 59 ½, whichever is *longer*.

This is how people screw themselves—they don't realize they have to keep making the withdrawals even after their pension and Social Security income start. In your case, because you have a pension coming, you would be receiving too much income once you reached age 59, and that could cause tax problems.

What I would recommend for you is something called the Rule of 55. The IRS says, "Hey you, if you leave your job in the calendar year that you turn 55 or later, you can withdraw money from your 401(k) without paying the 10 percent penalty."[23] You can leave your job for any reason—by getting laid off, fired, or even

---
23 IRS, Topic No. 558 Additional Tax on Early Distributions from Retirement Plans Other than IRAs, updated June 2021 https://www.irs.gov/taxtopics/tc558 Accessed 9/22/2012.

quitting. And if you're a public safety worker such as a police officer, you can leave even sooner, as early as age 50.[24]

But there are rules to the Rule of 55:

Unless you're a public safety worker, you can't use the rule the calendar year *before* you turn 55, and you can only withdraw funds from the 401(k) account with your most recent employer, not an account from several years back. The rule only applies to 401(k) accounts—if you roll the money into an IRA first, then you're screwed again because you can't use the rule. Instead, I suggest using the rule to take out the *portion* of your 401(k) that you need for income as one lump sum and get that money into a green bucket. Next, roll the rest of the 401(k) into an IRA. From there, you would use the two-bucket strategy to leverage a plan, thus defeating sequence risk.

Yes, you could leave 100 percent of your money in the 401(k) and still use the Rule of 55 to withdraw the income, but that would expose you to sequence risk. Of course, this recommendation comes without me having the benefit of examining your full situation, so please, never act on advice without first sitting down with a **fiduciary** who understands the rules and has your best interest at heart.

---

24 Ibid.

CHAPTER FOUR

PROTECT YOURSELF FROM BIG MARKET SWINGS

GET AN INCOME WITHOUT STRIKING OUT

"I've never heard a crowd boo a homer, but I've heard plenty of boos after a strikeout."

~ Babe Ruth

The Great Depression hit our country hard in October of 1929. One-quarter of the U.S. workforce was unemployed, more than a third of American cinemas closed, and America's favorite pastime was thrown a curveball. Major League Baseball attendance dropped by 40 percent and the average player's salary fell by 25 percent.[25] It was the worst economic downturn the country had ever seen, and yet, the legendary heavy-hitter Babe Ruth was doing all right.

It wasn't because he could still play baseball. In 1935 he was forced to retire. Baseball saw its heyday in the 20s when attendance skyrocketed, but during the Great Depression, athletes were impoverished and standing in bread lines. Not Babe. He had begun receiving regular income payments because he had invested well when he was earning the money.

---

[25] Cohen, Jennie, Baseball's First All-Star Game, History, Aug 2018. https://www.history.com/news/baseballs-first-all-star-game#:~:text=The%20Great%20Depression%20threw%20America's,salary%20fell%20by%2025%20percent. Accessed 5/7/2021.

This didn't happen by accident. It was said that Babe blew through his money during the Roaring 20s when he came into his glory days. This happens to a lot of athletes—they live high on the hog during their highest-earning years because for many of them, this is the most money they've ever seen in their lives. This was also true for Babe who grew up in a boys' home in the city of Baltimore. In 1922, when he was awarded a $52,000 contract worth the equivalent of about $800,000 today, he was just 27 years old. He had no idea what to do with this money other than spend it, but he did know how to recognize good advice.

This advice came from his business manager Christy Walsh who worried about Babe's future. At Walsh's urging, Babe went to see an insurance agent who convinced him to purchase a **deferred annuity**. With his World Series winnings and a portion of his annual salary, he invested in several annuity contracts. He had no way of knowing what would happen next—how the Roaring 20s would go out with a pitiful mew, how the market would crash, and how his career would end early when he started having health problems. His market investments, if he'd had any, would have been worthless during the Great Depression. But his annuities paid out.

It is reported that Babe Ruth received an income of $17,500 a year from his annuities, which would translate to an annual salary of more than $290,000 using 2020 dollars.[26]

Now, maybe you've heard about bad annuities and so you have a negative opinion about them. I understand—my grandfather felt the same way. This was my grandpa on my mother's side of the family who retired from Kirby without a pension. He liked that the annuity gave him a guaranteed monthly income, but he didn't like that it locked up his funds so that he could no longer get at his cash. When he died, the income continued to pay to my grandmother, but if there was any remaining balance in the account when she died—and I have no way of knowing if there was—then the account balance stayed with the insurance

---

26 Levan, Joh, Annuities are depression-proof; Babe Ruth knew the truth, Alliance America, July 2020. https://allianceam.com/income/Annuities-depression-proof-ask-Babe-Ruth. Accessed 5/06/2021.

company. Nobody likes the idea of giving their money away to an insurance company, and so a lot of people developed bad opinions about these kinds of annuities.

I'm here to tell you that annuities don't work like that anymore. I'd like to introduce you to the new kind of annuities you might think of as buffer accounts. These annuities do more than just take your money and turn it into an income. Remember the days I used to have to talk to my girlfriend on a phone with a long curly cord? Well, that kind of annuity—and the kind that my grandpa had—was like that wall phone with the cord. It tied you up!

Today, we have cell phones with a computer in our pocket, and we have annuities that allow you to profit when the market goes up without losing when the market goes down. These annuities also give you freedom to access your cash. That's the kind of technology you have at your disposal when you get into one of these newer annuities today. You don't even have to use it for income—not anymore.

In this chapter, I'm going to show you how to create a buffer account against risk so that you can protect your portfolio from big market swings.

Fast Fact: Annuities allow a retiree to spend at a level that investments alone would be unable to match without significant risk of running out of money before age 95.[27]

---

3 Places to Put Your Money

Whether you're a baseball Hall of Famer like Babe Ruth or a regular hardworking citizen like my grandfather, there are three places where you can put your money. I'm not going to tell you that any one place is wrong—truth is, for today's retirement, you're going to need a portion of your money in all three. Let's take a brief tour of these institutions and explore what they can help you accomplish during retirement.

---

27 Finke, Michael, and Pfau, Wade, New research from Principal shows annuities improve retirement outcomes, Principal National Life, April 2019. https://www.principal.com/about-us/news-room/news-releases/new-research-principal-shows-annuities-improve-retirement-outcomes Accessed 11/15/2021.

The Bank

Our first stop is the bank. Back in the 1980s when you could get an interest rate of 10 percent at your local bank, putting your money in certificates of deposits (CDs) was a good deal during retirement. Your money was right down the street from you, it was earning a rate of return that could beat inflation, and it was FDIC-insured for up to $250,000. You had no fear about losing this money because you weren't invested in the market, and you probably knew just about everyone who worked at your local branch.

The bank is still a safe place to put your money, but you know as well as I do that interest rates aren't paying very much anymore. What usually happens is that when interest rates on bank products go up, prices go up, too. Today, our economy continues to struggle in a post-pandemic world. As I write this, bank rates on savings accounts hover at around 0.05 percent, and even a five-year CD can't give you more than a 0.60 percent return. While it's true interest rates may be on the rise, the banks—although safe—can't help you beat inflation. The average rate of 3.22 percent doubles the price of things every 20 years, so think about what that will mean to you in retirement.[28]

What the bank can do for you is give you access to **liquidity**. Every retirement plan needs to include a place where cash reserves can be quickly accessed without penalty, market loss, or tax disruption. The bank is a good place to keep an emergency fund.

The Stock Market

The second place you can put your money is in market investments. You're probably familiar with these: stocks, bonds, mutual funds, **variable annuities**, ETFs, and so forth. Your stockbroker will tell you that the market is where you want to go if you want to earn as much interest as possible and keep up with inflation. And that's true.

---

[28] Historical Inflation Rates: 1914 – 2020, US Inflation Data, updated Jan. 2021. www.usinflationcalculator.com/inflation/historical-inflation-rates/. Accessed 2/9/2021.

But you also know the risks are different for somebody entering the retirement red zone. You've got the math of rebounds to contend with and the chance that sequence risk could strike. If you lose a portion of the money you need for your retirement income, your account may never recover. What the market does is completely outside of your control. The only thing you get to decide is what to do with this money.

Remember our two-bucket strategy? You can still keep a portion of your money in the stock market during retirement as long as you understand this money's timeline. For a market investment to average out its returns, you'll want to plan to leave it alone for at least 10 years. That means not accessing it regularly for income. By employing this strategy, you can reap the rewards of market returns, significantly reduce your risk, and increase your chances of success. For a refresher on how this works, head on over to Chapter 3.

Insurance Companies

The third place you can put your money is in insurance products such as annuities. An annuity in basic terms is a contract with an insurance company, but what you need to know is that annuities are the only financial vehicle capable of providing guaranteed income for life.[29] Our Chapter 2 directive was to "Think like a pensioner and not a gambler." How can you do that if you're not retiring with a pension from your employer?

The answer is the annuity. It can pay you an income for a certain number of years, for the rest of your life, or for the life of you and your spouse if that is what you want to do.

But this isn't all that an annuity can do. Even if you don't need an income, the kind of annuities I advocate for can provide you with a buffer account to protect you from big market swings. These accounts allow you to earn money when the market goes up without losing money when the market goes down. You get to earn returns without risk to your principal. That's right—you

---

29 Guarantees are backed by the financial strength of the claim's paying ability of the issuing company.

heard me correctly: your principal is 100 percent guaranteed not to drop due to market losses, while at the same time you have access to some of the market gains.[30] This allows your money to keep up with inflation without exposing it to the risk of loss.

Now, you're probably thinking that this is just too good to be true. Let me explain to you why it's not—it's too good not to do! The insurance company isn't going to allow you to earn 100 percent of what the market does; they'll only allow you to earn *some* of what the market does. For example, if the market went up 10 percent, you would get 60 percent of that. But the tradeoff is that when the market goes down by 10 percent, you keep 100 percent of what you've already gained. You don't go backwards or down!

In retirement, losses will hurt you more than gains will help you.

Having a buffer account that protects you from big market swings is especially important for someone stepping into the retirement red zone. Before you put even a toe over that line, remember: People aren't running out of money because they aren't earning high enough returns, they are running out because they're losing money at the wrong time. Just before and just after you retire are *the wrong times to lose*. An easy way to protect yourself against this risk is to transfer a portion of your retirement funds into one of these buffer accounts. When the contract is up, you can take the money back out and do with it what you want.

These contracts are, generally speaking, long-term commitments of five to 10 years, but you do have access to your funds. You can withdraw up to 10 percent annually without penalty as long as you're over the age of 59 ½—and this is an IRS rule, not the insurance company's rule. After the term of the contract is up, you can move this money out of the annuity and back into the stock market, or you can position it to give you income, or you can put it someplace else. The choice is yours to

---
30 Guarantees are based on the financial strength of the claim's paying ability of the issuing company.

make—just please, make your decision before the choice is made for you and the money is lost.

What Your Broker Won't Tell You

By now you're probably wondering, *Brian, if these buffer accounts are so freaking great, then why isn't my broker telling me about them?* That is exactly what I wanted to know when I first heard about them! But it makes sense if you think about it from the broker's point of view.

Imagine you have $1 million in your 401(k) being managed by a broker. If you tell them that you want a buffer account to protect against market risk, they will likely advise you to transition more than 40 percent of your portfolio into traditional safe-money investments such as bonds. This sounds like advice that follows the Rule of 100 that we talked about earlier, but it's not going to help the person in retirement. Here's why:

Bonds have an inverse relationship to interest rates. When interest rates fall, bond prices rise; when interest rates rise, bond prices fall. This is a phenomenon known as **interest rate risk** and it matters to someone retiring today. Why? Because looking out at a future that could span 20 to 30 years, there is only one way that interest rates could go. Take a look at the visual below.

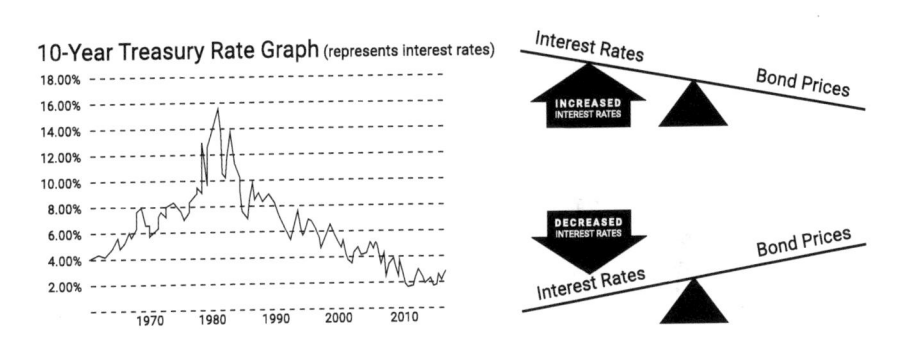

10-Year Treasury Rate Graph (represents interest rates)

Source: Macrotrends, 10 Year Treasury Rate - 54 Year Historical Chart

For the last 30 years, there has been a general trend of declining interest rates. We are currently experiencing one of the lowest interest rate environments the country has ever seen. If you're buying more bonds in a record-low interest rate environment, what's going to happen if you need to sell those bonds during a higher interest rate environment? They won't be worth as much. The regulatory authority FINRA warns, if you wanted to sell before your bond matures, "you'd likely have to sell at a price below face value."[31]

So now you understand why so many investors lost money in 2001 and again in 2008 when they were in their supposedly well-diversified portfolios that would protect them from risk. And now you're probably thinking, *Well, why can't my broker help me reallocate some of my money to an annuity buffer account?* The answer is that they are very limited in what they can sell.

Most brokerage firms do not sell the kinds of annuities that serve as a buffer against risk because those kinds of annuities do not invest directly in the stock market. The only annuities that your typical broker can get you are the variable kind that invest in the market, and these annuities expose your money directly to market risk.

Now, if a broker is receiving a fee or a commission for managing your money, and you want to get out of bonds and go into something that they don't have, then he or she is going to lose money. And that creates what we in the business call a conflict of interest.

Fast Fact: From 1953 to 1981 in an increasing interest rate environment, the average annual return for all bonds was 2.48%. From 1981 to 2018 in a decreasing interest rate environment, the average annual return for all bonds was 9.95%.[32]

---

[31] FINRA Staff, Bonds: Get a Handle on Your Risk: 5 Things To Know About Bond Duration, FINRA, April 20217, https://www.finra.org/investors/insights/get-handle-your-risk-5-things-know-about-bond-duration Accessed 11/15/2021.
[32] Damodaran, Aswath, Annual Returns on Stock, T.Bonds, and T.Bills: 1928 – Current, New York University, January 2019. http://pages.stern.nyu.edu/~adamodar/New_Home_Page/datafile/histretSP.html Accessed 10/01/2021.

3 Vehicles to Drive Your Income

Professional traders and big institutions never invest their money in the stock market without first protecting their downside. This means they peel off the money they know they need to protect, and they put it somewhere else. The only people who invest 100 percent of their money in the stock market are average investors trying like heck to save for retirement. And the reason they do it this way is because they aren't being taught how to do it better.

Now, you've learned how to avoid the danger of the retirement red zone. It's real simple: peel off the portion of your retirement funds that you want to protect and get it inside one of these buffer accounts. If you're still hung up about using an annuity, please take a minute to understand what kind of annuity I'm talking about. There are, generally speaking, three kinds of annuities: variable, immediate, and indexed. Not all of them can give you protection from market loss, so take a look at these with an eye for how they might help you protect your downside.

The Variable Kind

These annuities are exactly like they sound—they vary depending on the tweet of the day. If the market goes up, their value goes up. If the market goes down, their value goes down. Sure, variable annuities can be structured to produce a retirement income with some guarantees in place, but to do that, you'll have to pay a rider fee averaging 1 to 2 percent annually. Because they invest in the stock market, you'll also be paying expense ratio fees. To protect your income from the downside of market loss, variable annuities also have another fee called the M&E, which stands for mortality and expense, and is sometimes called the risk fee. The variable annuity is the only type of annuity to assess this risk fee, but please understand: even if you pay extra for income protection and guarantees, your account value can still lose principal. One benefit of the variable annuity, like all annuities, is that it grows tax-deferred.

Brokers like to tell you that these accounts will earn 4 to 7 percent regardless of what the market does—I've sat in on the meetings and heard them say this. But if that were true, I would personally have all of my money in an account like this, and I don't. What these annuities have are high fees and instability. These accounts have more strings attached than a puppet, but they can produce an income.

The Immediate Kind

This is the old-fashioned phone-on-the-wall-with-a-cord kind of annuity. It takes your money in one lump sum and turns it into a regular, reoccurring income. As its name suggests, this kind of annuity gives you the income right away—in as little as 30 days but no more than 13 months.[33] This can be a great thing if an immediate income is what you need.

The problem with the **immediate annuity** is that while it protects your money from market risk, it also keeps you tied to the wall, metaphorically speaking. Once you put your money into this type of annuity, you can't get it back out. If you want income and flexibility, or if you just want to create a buffer account against risk while you're in the red zone, then I have a better option for you.

The Indexed Kind

Also known in the industry as a fixed-indexed annuity, this type of account has a minimum fixed interest rate with an indexing option. You are not investing directly in the market; rather, you're tied to an index like the S&P 500. This allows you to receive some of the market gains with none of the market loss—AKA, downside protection. Here is how it works:

When the market index goes up, your account value goes up. You're not going to see double-digit returns like you do when you're directly invested in the market because the insurance company caps your gains. For example, if the market goes up by 10 percent, you might only get half that, which in this case would be 5 percent. The cap rates and indexes you get to choose

---

[33] FINRA Staff, Immediate Annuities: Money Now and for the Rest of Your Life... for a Price. April 2016. https://www.finra.org/investors/insights/immediate-annuities-money-now-and-rest-your-life. Accessed 5/7/2021.

from vary from company to company, but all of them give you principal protection, and in my opinion, that's the best tradeoff there is. In exchange for only receiving some of the gains, you are protected from ever receiving the loss. In other words, with an **indexed annuity**, you can't strike out.

The indexed annuity is also an example of a deferred annuity. It defers the income payment for five to 10 years or longer, during which time the account is allowed to grow protected from the big market swings. If you want to take your money out of the account early, before the contract time is up, you may face a **surrender charge**. But you will have access to up to 10 percent of your money annually without charge, provided you are of retirement age.

For example, let's say you have $100,000 in this buffer-account strategy. One day it happens that you need an extra $10,000 to put a new roof on your house. You call up the insurance company and ask them to send you a $10,000 check. And they do. Because this amount makes up no more than 10 percent of your account, there is no penalty and no surrender charge. You might owe taxes on this money depending on how the annuity was funded, but that's it.

With an immediate annuity, you would be out of luck.

This is why I call these vehicles buffer accounts. They give you a place to park a portion of your retirement funds while you are in the danger zone. Once the five to 10 to 12 years are over, the surrender charges end, and you're free to take this money out of the account and do with it whatever you want. Or, you can turn on an income provision and start receiving regular, reoccurring checks. Some indexed annuities also have provisions that allow for an increasing income to help address inflation.

Indexed annuities allow a retiree to spend at a level that investments alone would be unable to match without significant risk of running out of money before age 95.[34]

---

[34] Finke, Michael, and Pfau, Wade, New research from Principal shows annuities improve retirement outcomes, Principal National Life, April 2019. https://www.principal.com/about-us/news-room/news-releases/new-research-principal-shows-annuities-improve-retirement-outcomes Accessed 6/23/2021.

Studies also find that people with pensions are happier than those without. The indexed annuity is one way you can give yourself a pension if you don't have one, the income can increase over time, and any money left in the account can be passed to your family without probate. Whether you need the income or not, these buffer accounts can give you access to market gains without having to endure the uncertainty of market swings.

Up next: Find out how to keep the rest of your money in the market where it can grow using the newest algorithm technology, with its potential to enhance returns.

Uncommon Answers to Common Questions

Q&A Chapter 4

Q: When should I put money into an annuity? *I'm 55 years old and not yet ready to retire, but I know I won't be receiving a pension. Is it too early for me to put my money into an annuity?*

A: No. Now is the perfect time to put your money into one of these accounts because you will get a higher income for the same amount of money. If you understand how **delayed retirement credits** work for Social Security, then you get the idea. Most people know that if you wait to claim Social Security, you get a higher income—as much as 32 percent higher. This is the same actuarial math that the annuity companies use, based on life expectancy and interest rates, that pay a higher income if you wait.

A lot of people make the mistake of waiting to do real planning until they want the actual income. This is not in your best interest! The insurance company will reward you for putting in the money now and then waiting to take the income.

For example, if at age 55 you put $150,000 into an indexed annuity and then waited, you would be able to generate the same amount of income as the person who at age 62 put in $200,000.[35] There is no reason not to get a portion of your retirement money

---

[35] These numbers are hypothetical and do not represent the investment of actual funds nor the performance of an actual account.

protected and safe by using one of these buffer accounts. The only thing you want to be aware of when doing this is to choose your annuity based on what you need. If you need an income, even a small amount of income, you'll want to set up the deferred annuity ahead of time to turn this on for you at the appointed time.

CHAPTER FIVE

USE THE NEW TECHNOLOGY TO PROFIT FROM MARKET RETURNS

*"Once a new technology rolls over you,
if you're not part of the steamroller,
you're part of the road."*

~ Steward Brand

One day my neck was hurting and so during a break in my scheduled appointments, I set about doing a little google search for neck massagers. Not three days later, these catalogs start showing up in my mailbox: spa treatments, vitamins, heating pads—you name it. And I thought, *What the heck, is somebody spying on me?*

If you use Facebook or have an iPad, I'm sure you've experienced this same phenomenon. Facebook seems to know exactly what you're thinking. You share a post about how your granddaughter is making her first communion, and the next thing you know, ads for religious gifts start popping up. You order new guitar strings for your nephew's birthday, and suddenly, the ads on websites you visit are offering guitar books, chord charts, and tuners.

What the heck—is there a little man inside your iPad, like the man behind the curtain in *The Wizard of Oz?*

Nope. This kind of magic is done using a new technology called algorithms. Every time you scroll through pages and then slow down, these algorithms notice your behavior change, and they collect that data point. If you click on something, the algorithm collects that data again. It also gets smarter each time you scroll, so the knowledge it has about your behavior accumulates and preferences build. This is how it knows what ads and articles to send you—because you taught it based on your behavior.

Just as algorithms can determine which pages you're likely to linger on and what products you're likely to buy, they can also predict interest rates and market volatility based on investor behavior. These same kinds of data points are monitored and then programmed in to predict the movements of Wall Street. So, if you have an account being managed using this new technology, then these algorithms can sweep your money into the best asset classes based on the environment of any given day. If we're in a pandemic, if interest rates are falling, it can make the adjustments so you don't lose large amounts of cash.

The importance of keeping more of your profits is the subject of Chapter 5 because a true retirement plan doesn't just focus on earning the returns. **During retirement, it's not just about how much money you make, it's about how much money you keep.** This principle applies to all the ways we can lose our money: market loss, catastrophic illness, inflation, and taxation. Even a scarecrow with straw for brains can make money when the market is going up and the regular deposits are going into your accounts. But how to protect this money when the regular deposits are coming out of the account and the market is going haywire?

Now that's a horse of a different color.

Fast Fact: According to the World Economic Fund, the average 65-year-old American could outlive their retirement savings within nine years.[36]

---

3 Risks that Can Eat into Your Returns

We know several things can erode your wealth over time, and unexpected market loss is one of those things. Earlier in Chapter 2, we talked about how losing when you're in the retirement danger zone can mean game over for you during retirement. The

---
[36] Wood, Johnny, Retirees will outlive their savings by a decade, World Economic Forum, June 2019. https://www.weforum.org/agenda/2019/06/retirees-will-outlive-their-savings-by-a-decade/. Accessed 5/18/2021.

potential for market returns comes with a certain amount of risk, but if you apply the two-bucket strategy I talked about in Chapter 3 and keep the money you know you need for income separate, then you can give yourself a buffer account against this risk. This will protect your income from market risk, but what about the growth bucket? How can you protect those returns so that more of this money is yours to keep?

#1: Tax Risk

Perhaps the biggest threat to your nest egg is the train that people never see coming: taxation. Yes, earning market returns during retirement can help you pay for the higher taxes that are coming down the track. But a better directive, and what I help my clients to do, is to get your income as high as you can, as safely as you can, and as *tax-free* as you can.

If you're saving for retirement in accounts like the 401(k) or a **traditional IRA**, then you're getting a good deal on your taxes upfront. The federal government lets you save this money before you pay income taxes on it, and you don't even have to pay taxes on the growth. Until you go to take this money out, you don't have to think about taxes at all! And people like that.

But then come retirement, every dollar you spend is suddenly going to be subject to tax. How does that erode the spending power of your accounts?

Let's suppose you're retired, and you need to take out $10,000 a month for income. You're in a marginal tax bracket of around 20 percent, so what happens when you take out that $10,000? You're going to net $8,000. That's a 20 percent loss of income annually. Now, let's project forward by 10 years when tax rates go up. Now that same $10,000 withdrawal is only going to net you $6,000. That's an even bigger pay cut! And when you add inflation on top of that, you can see the disaster ahead on the tracks.

There are two taxes we all pay on our income: federal and state. The state of Pennsylvania doesn't tax your pension income or the money coming out of retirement accounts, and that's nice. But the savings are small compared to your federal tax bill because here's what you need to know.

First, understand why I'm so confident tax rates will go up. The highest marginal tax rates for 2021 are at 37 percent—an historic low. The highest rate ever seen was 94 percent at the end of World War II, and it remained high—in the 90 to 50 percent range—until it went down to 38.5 percent in 1987.[37] The provisions of the Tax Cuts and Jobs Act of 2017 that set our historic 37 percent rate will expire on December 31, 2025, when tax brackets are scheduled to revert to 2017 levels.[38] The 2017 levels are *higher* for five out of the seven income tax brackets, so most people will see an increase to their tax bill in the coming years unless provisions are extended.[39]

If that isn't enough to convince you, we need to do something to save Social Security. The projected shortages to the program have worsened since the pandemic during which millions of Americans filed for unemployment and stopped contributing to the system. The reserves will become depleted in 2035, at which time continuing income would be sufficient to pay only 76 percent of scheduled benefits unless changes are made.[40]

The next visual shows you where we've been and where we are now. So ask yourself, during your 20-to-30-year retirement, which direction do you think taxes will go? Down, or up?

---

37 Tax Policy Center, Historical Highest Marginal Income Tax Rates, Feb 2020. https://www.taxpolicycenter.org/statistics/historical-highest-marginal-income-tax-rates. Accessed 5/10/2021.
38 El-Sibaie, Amir, A Look Ahead at Expiring Tax Provisions, Tax Foundation, January 2018 https://taxfoundation.org/look-ahead-expiring-tax-provisions Accessed 11/15/2021.
39 Ibid.
40 Social Security and Medicare Boards of Trustees, A Summary of the 2020 Annual Reports, 2020. https://www.ssa.gov/oact/trsum/. Accessed 5/10/2021.

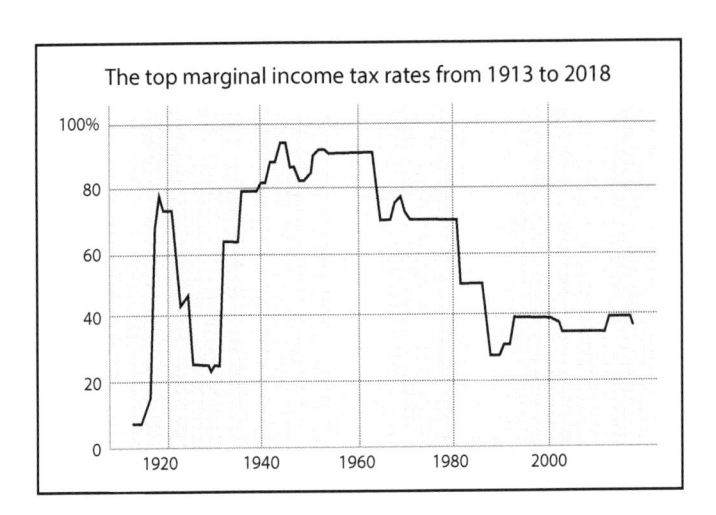

The top marginal income tax rates from 1913 to 2018

Source: Urban-Brookings Tax Policy Center. Statistics. "Historic Individual Income Tax Parameters: 1913 to 2018."

I often tell people if you wait to do your tax planning until you're retired, it might already be too late. Tax paying is what you do when you have no choice. This is where having a true retirement plan with a growth strategy can help mitigate the effects of tax risk.

If you act early and get a written plan, it's possible to reposition the money in your taxable accounts so that during the second half of retirement, when your healthcare costs are high and your tax rates are even higher, you're withdrawing income from accounts that give you this income tax-free.

During your working years, if your taxes are low, it usually means that your income is also low. Rather than clipping your income in retirement, a better strategy is to get as much of this income from tax-free accounts as possible. A **Roth IRA** is one such example of a tax-free account. Any money you put in there is allowed to grow and compound its interest tax-free so that when you go to access this money, there is no tax bill to pay. The income from a Roth is also not used against you to calculate your taxable income for Social Security, and with a Roth, there is no RMD to withdraw.

The sooner you focus on a strategy that includes these types of accounts, the more likely you'll be able to access tax-free income. The key is having a written plan. With tax planning, we can make these projections happen on paper to see what the costs and benefits would be before you take action.

> **Fast Fact:** A survey of retirees ages 62 to 75 with annual household incomes greater than $100,000 revealed that taxes made up more than 31% of overall spending.[41]

#2: Long-Term Care Risk

A health event is another thing that people miss when they work with a broker who doesn't understand how to take the money out. What happens when you're living on a relatively fixed income, and suddenly you need to take out more money from your account than just a fixed percent? If you're relying only on market investments, then you might have to sell at a loss. Furthermore, you'll owe more taxes on this money, which means you'll have to withdraw even more money. And how long can your accounts continue to support these large withdrawals without a long-term growth strategy in place?

Your broker might tell you not to worry about this risk. After all, traditional long-term care insurance is expensive, and nobody wants to believe they will ever need it. At the root of this problem is the number of Americans who remain in denial about how long they will live. **Two out of every three men underestimate how long a 65-year-old man will live in retirement while half of all women are guilty of the same thing.**[42] And yet it's women who are affected most by long-term care risk. Because they tend to be younger than their spouse and live, on average, five years longer, it often happens that they spend down the retirement accounts

---

[41] Lincoln Financial Group, "The underrated impact of taxes on retirement – Research Study," 2010; Order code: LFG-TAX-WPR001. https://www.pdffiller.com/482878806--The-underrated-impact- Accessed 10/01/2021.
[42] The Longevity Project, Lifetime Income to Support Longer Life: Retirement Innovation in the New Age of Longevity. In collaboration with the Principal Financial Group, 2020. https://secure02.principal.com/publicvsupply/GetFile?fm=RF2513&ty=VOP. Accessed 5/18/2021.

while taking care of their husband.[43] By the time they need care, there's no money left.

The longer we live, the more our bodies age and change. Long-term care costs don't just refer to the roughly $10,000 a month you'll spend if you have to go to a nursing home in the state of Pennsylvania; they can also refer to homemaker services such as cleaning or cooking meals, and community living facilities for adults who need some health services but not round-the-clock care. These costs can range anywhere from $1,500 to $4,600 a month.[44] By getting a growth strategy in place, you can be assured that the buckets for your later income needs are kept full and replenished regularly.

Fast Fact: More than half of all women 65 and older will need some form of long-term care, and they will need it for an average of 2.5 years.[45]

#3: Inflation Risk

Back in my grandfather's days, retirement didn't last long enough for inflation to be that big of a concern. In 1950, little more than half of all men made it to age 65, and if they did, the average length of retirement was 13 years.[46] **Now, with men expected to live to 84 and women to age 86, the average retiree will need their retirement savings to last 20 years or longer once they hit age 65.**[47]

So let me ask you: If prices roughly double every 20 years, how are you going to fill this gaping income hole?

The majority of advisory firms will answer this question by showing you colorful charts with graphs and pies that give

---

43 Kockanek, Kenneth D.; Jiaquan, Xu; Arias, Elizabeth, Mortality in the United States, 2019. National Center for Health Statistics, Centers for Disease Control and Prevention, December 2020. https://www.cdc.gov/nchs/products/databriefs/db395.htm. Accessed 4/07/2021.
44 Genworth Cost of Care Survey, Monthly Media Costs: Pennsylvania – State (2020). https://www.genworth.com/aging-and-you/finances/cost-of-care.html. Accessed 5/18/2021.
45 Benz, Christine, 75 Must-Know Statistics About Long-Term Care: 2018 Edition, Morningstar, August 2018. https://www.morningstar.com/articles/879494/75-must-know-statistics-about-long-term-care-2018-edition. Accessed 5/18/2021.
46 Social Security History: Life Expectancy for Social Security. https://www.ssa.gov/history/lifeexpect.html. Accessed 6/17/2021.
47 Social Security Administration, "Benefits Planner: Life Expectancy." https//www.ssa.gov/planners/lifeexpectancy.html. Accessed 5/25/2021.

statistics and returns, without ever giving you an actual plan. What I've learned over the years is that it's the simple things in life that are the most powerful. A written plan has power. It can show you in black and white exactly what your income will be now, and what it will be in 20 years when everything costs a lot more.

For some retirees, if their investments keep up with inflation, they will meet their income goal. For others, more aggressive allocations may be required. We already talked about the retirement red zone back in Chapter 2, when we saw how two siblings could retire with the same amount of money earning the same rate of return, and yet not have the same amount of security. So how can you stay in the market during retirement without losing your shirt?

Sequence risk cannot be removed from your portfolio until you split the money up between safe money and risk money. In Chapter 3, I showed you how to do this using a two-bucket strategy. In Chapter 4, I showed you how to choose from among your safe-money options. Now, in Chapter 5, I'm going to show you how you can more effectively manage your risk bucket by taking advantage of the new technology.

Fast Fact: *Over a 20-year retirement, an increase of just 1% to the inflation rate would decrease your income by $34,406; an increase of 3% would decrease income by $117,000.*[48]

The Truth About Money Managers

Traditional asset allocation has you splitting up a sum of money between different asset classes. You have your large-cap, your mid-cap, and your small-cap stocks; you have your domestic and international stocks; you have your fixed-income bonds. This way of investing over time gives you an overall trending line upwards. The problem? None of those positions are talking to each other.

---

[48] LIMRA, Even When Inflation is Low, it's Higher for Retirees, April 2016. https://www.limra.com/en/newsroom/industry-trends/2016/even-when-inflation-is-low-its-higher-for-retirees/ Accessed 8/11/2021.

Imagine an asset class that is not performing well. In order for you to be in the best asset class at the best time, you need to sell off the asset class that's performing poorly at the right time, based on the right economic indicators, and get into the asset class that is performing. Now here is where I will take you behind the metaphorical curtain to see what happens next.

Most people think that if they have a poorly-performing asset and an advisor who is managing the money, then that is what he or she is doing: They are selling the assets to move you out of poorly-performing positions and into better-performing ones at just the right moment in time.

Well, I am very sorry to have to be the one to tell you that in most cases, this is not what's happening. Today's global market positions trade way too quickly. Imagine you're an advisor with 45 clients to manage. It is difficult, nay, impossible, to keep up with the economic cycles these days given how fast the market moves. It can't be done—there isn't an advisor on earth who can get your money in and out fast enough, and even if they could, they'd be accused of churning, which as I talked about in the introduction is a violation of SEC rules. And if mutual funds happen to be one of the asset classes you're in, then rule 35d-1would apply, which also prevents the advisor from getting you out of poor funds.

Today's markets are much more dynamic. They move up and down rapidly—it's nothing for us to see a 1,000-point swing in a single day. The old technology for managing this money was the buying and selling of assets, but that's the old wall phone with the long curly cord. Today, we have a better way.

Today, roughly 70 percent of the market is being traded by algorithms. If you understand how Facebook is spying on you, then you understand algorithms. They work for you 24 hours a day, seven days a week. They can rapidly move your money from one asset class into another to constantly maximize your gains and minimize your loss. Now, the positions are talking to each other. Now, the positions are moving on a minute-by-minute basis, and nobody gets in trouble with the SEC. This is how you stay ahead during the market conditions of today.

Wall phones, cordless phones, or smartphones—how will you dial into returns once you enter the red zone and loss matters? If you use the technology provided by the newer cell phones, then your long-term risk bucket can stay replenished by benefiting from the technology of algorithms.

> **Fast Fact:** *"In the past 30 years our markets have undergone a sweeping transformation and many of our rules, regulations, and requirements have, understandably, become outdated." ~ Jay Clayton, Chairman of the SEC*[49]

Uncommon Answers to Common Questions

Q&A Chapter 5

Q: When is a good time to begin tax planning? *I'm retired at age 65 and I've got half a million dollars sitting in my IRA. I've also got a pension, too, so I don't need to touch my IRA. My wife and I want to leave it to our children. I know that in seven years when I turn 72, I'm going to have to start taking my required minimum distribution (RMD) from my IRA. So, my question is, when should I start doing tax planning? Do I wait until I start taking my RMD? Or do I start now? And what exactly should I do to preserve as much of this money as possible?*

Now is the time to start tax planning. Now is always going to be the answer to this particular question because by the time it comes to pay the taxes owed, it's usually too late to do anything. Let's look at the specifics of your situation.

With a proper growth strategy, that half-million you have in your IRA has the potential to roughly double by the time you have to take your RMD. When that happens, you'll be forced to withdraw more money from the account, paying taxes on an income you don't need. At age 72, if you're withdrawing an extra $25,000 to $30,000 a year, that's going to compound your tax

---

[49] U.S. Securities and Exchange Commission, Agency Finance Report, Fiscal Year 2020. https://www.sec.gov/files/sec-2020-agency-financial-report_1.pdf. Accessed 5/21/2021.

problems. Now, not only will you have to pay taxes on the income that comes from a qualified account, but this withdrawal could also impact the amount of taxation you have to pay on your other income and your Social Security check. It could also increase your tax rate. I see it happen all the time—the RMD bumps people up into a higher income tax bracket. The increase from the 12 percent to the 22 percent tax bracket is an increase of 84 percent. Is this really how you want to spend your IRA money?

The good news is that the IRS doesn't require you to take your RMD distribution until age 72. That means you have seven years to do some real tax planning. This is a great opportunity. Taxes will almost always be higher in the future. Why not pull income from the taxable bucket during the first phrase of your retirement to convert half of it into the tax-free bucket for phase two? That will decrease the amount of your RMD withdrawals so that when tax rates rise, more of this money will be received by your heirs tax-free.

CHAPTER SIX

HOW TO FIRE YOUR ADVISOR AND HIRE A TEAM

> *"The way a team plays as a whole determines its success. You may have the greatest bunch of individual stars in the world, but if they don't play together, the club won't be worth a dime."*
>
> ~ Babe Ruth

When it hit me, the awareness made me so uncomfortable—I remember the moment like it was yesterday. I was meeting with my accountant on behalf of my firm, we were sitting in her office with the framed poster of the Pittsburgh Steelers on the wall. I had asked her a question about a tax strategy I'd learned from a colleague, and she replied, "Oh sure. Yes, you could do that." And I thought to myself, *Why am I always the one coming up with the ideas?*

I had thought this before. I'd found myself wondering every time we would meet, *Why isn't there a comprehensive checklist to follow? A system in place? A team working on my behalf?* I would leave the meeting wondering how could I know with any certainty that every I was dotted and every T crossed?

I knew in my gut that it was time for us to end our professional relationship, but every time I went in to see her, I couldn't do it.

"Oh hi, Brian!" she would say whenever I saw her. "How are you doing? How is your brother? How is your mom? Oh, she's such a nice lady."

And I was like, *Oh, she's such a nice person! I can't fire her!* And I would totally chicken out.

By this point in the book, you might have realized that you're working with the wrong advisor. If you're newly retired, or retirement is 10 to 15 years away, and you're not working with someone who specializes in the distribution of your assets, then you probably don't have a true plan. Problem is, you might like your advisor. You might even care about this person! I know exactly how you feel. I had the same kind of relationship with my accountant.

Back when I first founded Secure Money Advisors, I took my taxes to my college accounting professor. She was a great teacher and a wonderful person. I had benefitted so much from being in her class, and I trusted her and knew she would take care of me and my firm. I thought I would never have to hire another accountant again for as long as I lived.

But then my company grew. And as it continued to grow, I knew in my heart I wasn't getting the kind of comprehensive planning advice I needed to address the tax complexities of a company this size.

You might also be facing the same kind of issue with your current advisor. When I ask prospective clients about their taxes, about filing for Social Security, they look at me confused. "My current advisor doesn't do any of that." And that's when one of two things happens. Either the light bulb goes on and they realize they're working with the wrong guy, or they find themselves defending this person. When I show them other financial opportunities and where they might be missing out, they start to feel even worse.

Now, you might be working with an advisor who does specialize in the distribution phase, and you might already have a true plan. How can you tell? One of the key indicators will be how you feel when things happen outside of your control—things like market turbulence, job loss, and worldwide pandemics. If your life can go on just the same without any change to your income, then you've got a true plan. If you're watching the market, losing sleep, and putting plans on hold, then you probably don't have a true plan.

> **Fast Fact:** According to the 2020 EBRI Report, nearly half of all retirees surveyed said they retired earlier than planned.[50]

The 5 Functions of a Retirement Plan

Most people know how to tell time, but they don't know what all goes inside a watch. And that's okay. You don't need to understand how the mechanism works in order to get yourself to places on time. If you can read the watch, you can tell the time, even if you don't understand exactly how the watch works.

A true retirement plan is just like that. You might not have a full understanding of how algorithms work, how the index operates, or what the tax rates and thresholds are any given year, but you will understand what the plan does. You'll know how it helps you maintain your independence. You'll know how it will allow you to do all the things you want to be doing during retirement. You'll know you have a true plan based on how it functions, what it does, and how that makes you feel. What follows are the five functions of a true retirement plan.

Function #1: To provide an income.

If there is one concern people share with me more than any other, it's the fear of running out of money. This fear is especially acute if you don't have a pension, but even if you do have a pension, you'll still want to know that the money won't run out. The basic function of any true retirement plan, then, is to provide an income, either for a certain person, a certain time, or the rest of your life.

If you're the kind of retiree who has a pension, then you'll want to ask yourself, *Do I need this income for one life or two?* If you're married and your spouse doesn't have a pension, then you'll want

---
[50] Employee Benefit Research Institute, Key Findings of the 30th Annual Retirement Confidence Survey, May 2020. https://www.ebri.org/docs/default-source/webinars/rcs2020_webinarslides.pdf?s-fvrsn=b0a33d2f_4. Accessed 5/27/2021.

to take steps to ensure the income will continue when you pass away. Does the pension go with you when you pass away like your Social Security check will?

Your retirement plan will also need to adapt and respond to other events outside of your control. What if your pension terms change or the company goes bankrupt? What if you retire early? How will you fund the income gap while waiting for Social Security and Medicare to kick in?

If you are the kind of retiree who doesn't have a pension, then you need to create all of the income not covered by Social Security. And if you're married, then you'll also need to think about funding this income for your spouse, because when one spouse passes away, one of the Social Security income checks goes with them.

You'll also want to look at how you're positioned for market risk. If the market takes a plunge just before or after you retire, you'll want to know that the income you're supposed to receive will stay the same. You'll need a strategy to accomplish what I consider the golden retirement planning rule: **Get that income as high as you can, as safely as you can, and as tax-free as you can.** Having a plan allows you to achieve that.

Function #2: To provide written proof.

Last week I had a couple come into my office and tell me a story about how they had gone to the grocery store together. They did their shopping, loaded the bags into the trunk of the car, and drove home. They opened the garage door, pulled in, and went into the house. The wife made dinner, the husband fed the cat. They had a nice meal, watched some television, and went to bed.

It was only when they woke up in the morning that they remembered the groceries sitting in the trunk of the car!

It's no big secret that as we get older, our short-term memory might not be as sharp as it used to be. Take a minute and think about the current plan your advisor has provided for you. Do you remember what you discussed? Do you know how much income you'll be receiving and when? Is there anything in writing, in black and white, where it says exactly what your retirement income will be each year, in five years, in 10 years?

Don't expect yourself to memorize all of this! It should be written down. You should also know how the income will be protected from inflation and market loss, and how much in taxes you will have to pay and when. And, finally, you'll want to know how the income will continue even after the loss of a spouse.

A true plan will show you in writing how much money you'll have and when, so you'll have peace of mind knowing that you won't run out.

Function #3: To provide a tax plan.

Another thing to ask about is taxes. If you have a retirement account, then you'll owe taxes on the money you take out for income. This is true for your 401(k), 403(b), and 457 plans as well as your traditional IRAs. Where is the money going to come from to pay this tax bill? And what about the taxes on your Social Security income? Have you and your advisor looked at your options for getting this income as high as you can and as tax-free as you can?

Studies find that a tax-efficient withdrawal strategy can add more than six years to the life of your portfolio compared to a tax-inefficient strategy.[51] Think about how much in returns you'd have to earn and how much risk you'd have to take to extend your portfolio by six years, and you'll understand the value of getting a tax-efficient plan.

---

51 Cook, Kristen A.; Meyer, William; Reichenstein, William, Tax-Efficient Withdrawal Strategies, Financial Analysts Journal, December 2018. https://www.tandfonline.com/doi/abs/10.2469/faj.v71.n2.2 Accessed 6/28/2021.

Function #4: To organize everything all in one place.

The reality is simple: Today's retirement has gotten longer, the world has gotten more complicated, and the old way of doing things might not protect you from running out of money. A true retirement plan must address these five areas: income, investment efficiency, taxation, healthcare, and legacy planning. Your advisor should be asking you about taxes, income, market risk, Social Security, and an RMD strategy. They should be talking to you about the most efficient way you can take this money out of the accounts because to just keep it growing isn't going to be good enough.

At my firm, not only do we provide a written plan, but we also help to get your entire financial life organized so that everything you need lives in one, safe place. We package all our clients' documents together in binders to help them stay organized, and we update the plan regularly.

As your life changes, your plan needs to evolve with you. If you get married, have a new grandchild, or decide to sell a home or start a business, these things will affect your taxes, your income, your wishes, and desires. **Your advisor should set up recurring appointments with you to review the plan at regular intervals to make sure your investments stay on track.**

Function #5: To instruct your heirs on how to carry out your legacy.

When it's your time to move to the next phase, you'll want to make things as easy as possible for the people behind you. This might include end-of-life decisions spelled out in a **healthcare directive** giving instructions to your doctor and medical staff so your family doesn't have to make these decisions. It might also include a **healthcare power of attorney**, a will, or a **trust**. At my firm, our plan package also includes exclusive material that will help your loved ones carry out these wishes. When you have a true plan, all the information anyone could need will all be in one place.

We always suggest letting at least one of your beneficiaries know about this plan—where it lives and what it includes—so that they can step in to help if you need assistance or something happens to you.

When you boil everything down, what I want you to have in your plan is growth, control, and safety. And just like a watch that can help you stay on time, having a written plan can also help you get peace of mind. A written plan, something that you can hold in your hands, can show you with certainty that your retirement is on track to give you the income you need to maintain the lifestyle you've earned. It will also ensure your legacy instructions will be carried out as you wish. In short, a true retirement plan is what you can look at and read to know that things will be okay.

> *Fast Fact: When workers with benefit plans were asked what would be the most valuable improvement, the most-cited response was explanations for how much income their savings would produce and whether they were on track for retirement.*[52]

Keep Your Plan on Track

It's easy for someone in an office wearing a suit and a tie to talk to you about losing money when the money isn't theirs to lose. I know because that job used to be mine, but it never did sit well with me. I couldn't do it, and I left the brokerage firm where I worked because I knew in my gut there had to be a better way.

I left and read every book I could get my hands on about retirement planning. I talked to my colleagues, attended seminars, did research. When I found that better way, I founded Secure Money Advisors and never looked back.

Aside from the complexities addressed by having a true plan, there are other qualities you'll want to look for in an advisor. One of the most important ones isn't a buzzword in today's media, yet it's important to everyone for more reasons than one. That word: independence.

---

[52] Ibid.

Two kinds of agents

Yes, a true plan can give you financial independence, including a way to provide and pay for your long-term healthcare needs. But what I'm talking about here is the independence of the advisor you're working with. In our industry, there are two kinds of financial professionals: **captive agents** and **independent agents**.

Captive agents work for a big firm, company, or bank. You'll probably recognize the name of the firm, it will be a name that everybody knows, and it might even be nationwide. While it can give a person a sense of security to know that the company where they have their money invested is famous, working with a captive agent during retirement has several disadvantages.

First, those name-brand, proprietary investments that the advisor made sound so glamorous are probably the only kind of investments the advisor can sell. They have to work from a limited menu, and while the stuff on the menu might sound good, it's still limited when you consider the hundreds of thousands of options out there.

Second, the investment menu is typically designed for the person who is growing their funds to *save* for retirement. What you need are products and solutions that can help you distribute your funds, AKA, *spend* in retirement. To continue with our menu analogy, it's great that the captive agent can offer you a selection of really great hamburgers, but what if what you need is a nice grilled piece of chicken or fish? This is the difference between working with someone who specializes in your **distribution years** (retirement) versus your **accumulation years** (when you are working).

Two kinds of standards

And lastly, the captive agent might have a conflict of interest. Sure, a nice greasy hamburger might taste good, but is it really good for you, or good for them? Most captive agents operate under **suitability standards** rather than serving as your fiduciary.

"Fiduciary" is a buzzword in the financial industry you have probably heard before. A fiduciary is a professional sworn to a duty of care, trust, and loyalty. It's the highest standard in the financial industry, and it requires that an advisor serves in the best interest of the client at all times.[53] Even if it causes them to lose money, even if they'll receive a lower commission for the recommendation they make, if it's better for you, then the advisor must recommend it according to the fiduciary standard. This can be a wonderful thing—I myself have chosen to hold myself to the fiduciary standard of care. But with captive agents, you don't always know if they are *acting* as your fiduciary, so this is a question you'll want to ask them.

Instead of serving in the best interest of the client, the suitability standard requires only that the advisor reasonably believe that their recommendations are suitable. As long as the product can reasonably help the investor achieve his or her objectives, they aren't required to tell you about the better options that exist. This can create a conflict of interest for someone at or near retirement. Let's look at this in terms of the person who needs a nice grilled piece of chicken or fish.

The Chicken Nuggets of the Financial World

If the suitability standard sounds a bit fuzzy to you, it's because it is. This becomes especially obvious when it comes to offering annuities. Back in Chapter 4 when we covered different types of annuities, I expressed my opinion and gave you the facts about variable annuities. This is where the fiduciary standard becomes vital to keeping your retirement on the right track.

If you tell an advisor, "I need something that can give me an income in retirement," and they aren't acting as your fiduciary, they could recommend a variable annuity. A variable annuity, in this case, is suitable: it can give you an income.

But. It also comes with charges, expense ratios, and the M&E fee—something no other kind of annuity has. If you want it to give you an income, then in most cases you must pay for

---

[53] Securities and Exchange Commission, Commission Interpretation Regarding Standard of Conduct for Investment Advisers, July 2019. https://www.sec.gov/rules/interp/2019/ia-5248.pdf. Accessed 5/27/2021.

an income rider—and that can add another 1 to 2 percent fee annually. All of these fees are weighted directly against those stock market returns.

To continue with our menu metaphor, if annuities are like chicken, you might say that variable annuities are the chicken nuggets of the financial world. Sure, they're technically still considered chicken even though they've been separated, breaded, and fried. Sure, they come with dippin' sauce and taste freaking great with fries. But are they really good for you? Are chicken nuggets in your best interest? Can they sustain you for the next 20 to 30 years if healthier, cheaper, and better options exist?

Don't you want to know about these other options? The independent agent can get you access to them—all of them, even variable annuities if chicken nuggets are what you want. The captive agent cannot.

Okay, who's hungry? Did someone say, "Lunch?"

Fast Fact: Chicken McNuggets were invented in the 1950s, they are the highest-calorie item on the menu, and nutritionists agree they're one of the reasons obesity and health problems are such a problem in the U.S., especially among children.[54]

What to Expect from an Independent Fiduciary

Our tendency as human beings is to seek validation. We like it when people agree with us, and when they tell us what we want to hear, we walk away feeling good. But that feeling can fade pretty quick after you walk out of the room. This is what happened to me every time I met with my teacher friend the accountant. This is also what makes my job so tricky: as an advisor held to the fiduciary standard, my job is to tell you what you *need* to hear, which isn't always what you *want* to hear.

Most people know deep down inside what they should do with their money. They know they need a true plan, and they

---

[54] Laliberte, Marissa, 12 Things You Probably Didn't Know About McDonald's McNuggets, Reader's Digest, May 2020. https://www.rd.com/list/mcdonalds-chicken-mcnugget-facts/. And Chicken nuggets Facts for Kids, Kiddie Encyclopedia, https://kids.kiddle.co/Chicken_nuggets. Accessed 5/27/2021.

know they need to get organized. So, they set up a meeting with a financial professional. How can you tell if this person is acting as your fiduciary? One of the first clues will be how they conduct their first meeting. It shouldn't be about products and investments; it should be about you.

Before diving into investments and solutions, the fiduciary professional will want to sit with you and have a nice conversation. He or she will ask questions designed to get an idea of who you are, who you want to take care of, and what you want your retirement to look like. This might include talking about family members, houses, or a bucket list of the things you want to do. You can expect this first meeting to last anywhere from 45 to 60 minutes during which time you'll have the opportunity to discuss your retirement goals.

Next, the fiduciary will take a look at your investments and retirement income sources to determine if the accounts you have match up with your needs and goals. At my firm, if we're getting along and it feels like we are a good fit, then our team will move forward with creating a true retirement plan. This plan will meet your needs and shape your path to keep you moving ahead and on the right track to meet those goals.

And lastly, an independent advisor serving in the fiduciary capacity will also give you access to other professionals that he or she feels uphold the same standards to help you get what you need. Like myself, they will work with attorneys, tax advisors, or Medicare specialists who either work right there in the office or down the street. They can make referrals to a great real estate agent if you need to sell property or a car salesman if you need to buy a new vehicle; they can even help you file for your Social Security. **In short, the independent advisors are the people who truly care.** They're not loyal to the big company they work for, they are loyal to you, the client they serve.

When planning for retirement, it's not always about the person with the best personality, the biggest office, the snazziest suit; it's about the person who can and will give you the best advice.

And I believe that after working a lifetime to save this money, you deserve the very best advice.

How many of us stay in bad relationships because it's so hard to break up? I know I once stayed with a girl because she was so sweet, I just didn't have the heart. That was the worst thing I could have done because, in the end, staying with her longer only meant I hurt her more. When you work with the wrong advisor, the person you are hurting is you.

Fast Fact: Two out of every 10 retirees say they don't know who to go to for financial and retirement planning advice.[55]

Uncommon Answers to Common Questions
Q&A Chapter 6

Q: Where can I find an independent fiduciary advisor?

Hello! I'm right here. My name is Brian Quaranta, and as the president and founder of Secure Money Advisors, I'm proud of the number of people who we have helped to retire happily and securely. Not a day goes by that I don't hear stories from my clients about the time they're spending with their grandkids, the cruises they're taking, or the hobbies they've picked up since retirement. I love hearing their stories, and I am confident that with a little planning, we can help you accomplish those same goals.

As a special gift to you, my reader, I am offering a complimentary, no-obligation portfolio review with either myself or one of the fiduciary advisors on my team. Sit down with us and let us know what's on your mind.

Retirement planning doesn't have to be complicated. What I want for you is what I want for all my clients: to have peace of mind and certainty knowing that every I is dotted and every T crossed; to have confidence that the money won't run out because

---

55 Employee Benefit Research Institute (EBRI), with Greenwald Research, 2021 Retirement Confidence Survey, 2021. https://www.ebri.org/docs/default-source/rcs/2021-rcs/2021-rcs-summary-report.pdf?sfvrsn=b-d83a2f_2 Accessed 6/02/2021.

you have a plan that's so simple and easy to understand, you can explain it to somebody as easily as you can tell the time on a watch.

Schedule your complimentary, no-obligation portfolio review by calling 724- 382-1298, or email us directly at info@securemoneyadvisors, or go to https://www.securemoneyadvisors.com/contact/.

We look forward to helping you get a true plan to keep your retirement on the right track.

ABOUT THE AUTHOR

After getting into the financial business during one of the worst decades on Wall Street, Brian Quaranta went on to build a retirement planning firm with a focus on safety, protection, and cash flow. As founder and president of Secure Money Advisors, he takes pride in his firm's unique space in the marketplace as an independent agency. Staffed by a team of fiduciaries, Secure Money Advisors serves the residents of Pittsburgh and Western Pennsylvania by giving them access to both tactical market investments and safe money options.

As a young boy growing up, Brian saw how quickly things changed for his family when the company where his father worked went bankrupt. Determined to learn everything he could about money, Brian received a scholarship to Robert Morris University where he graduated with a BA in business and finance. Now, as an investment advisor representative with over 20 years of experience, he holds his Series 65 securities license in addition to being a licensed insurance agent. He adheres to the fiduciary standard of care, is a member of the National Ethics Association, and has trained under America's IRA distribution expert, Ed Slott.

As a sought-after retirement educator and planning expert, Brian hosts the *On the Money with Secure Money* radio segment airing Saturday mornings on 94.5 FM 3WS, 100.1 FM & 1020 AM KDKA, as well as local stations. His television show, *On the Money with Secure Money*, airs weekends throughout the region.

When not in the office or the studio filming, Brian can be found spending time with his wife Katie and their two sons in the Wexford area. He stays active during his free time with skiing, traveling, and the building and flying of remote-control model planes.

Glossary of Terms

ACCUMULATION YEARS – The financial phase during your working years when you are saving and growing your assets.

BENEFICIARY – An individual entitled to collect assets as decreed by a written, legal document.

BUY-AND-HOLD STRATEGY – A passive investment strategy whereby market investments are bought and then held for a long period regardless of market fluctuations, so investors capture 100 percent of market gains and 100 percent of market loss.

COST-OF-LIVING ADJUSTMENT (COLA) – Paycheck adjustments that give claimants of Social Security a way to keep pace with inflation and the rising price of goods and services.

DEFERRED ANNUITY – An annuity that promises to pay the owner a regular income, either as a lump sum or as a lifetime stream, at some future date.

DELAYED RETIREMENT CREDITS (DRCs) – Credits used to increase the amount of your Social Security benefit during the period beginning with the month you achieve full retirement age and ending with the month you turn age 70.

DISTRIBUTION YEARS – The financial phase during your non-working years when you are spending the assets you saved.

DIVERSIFICATION – A strategy for risk management that relies on a wide variety of market investments mixed within a portfolio.

LEGACY PLANNING – The simple process of transferring your stuff to someone else, including the transfer of assets, obligations, or responsibilities that may include end-of-life decisions

FIDUCIARY – A professional who holds a legal or ethical relationship of trust to prudently take care of money or other assets for another person.

HEALTHCARE POWER OF ATTORNEY – A written document in which you name someone (your "agent" or "attorney-in-fact") to make healthcare decisions for you if you are unable to speak for yourself. This person is then able to act on your behalf and carry out your directions for healthcare, without the delays of court proceedings.

HEALTHCARE DIRECTIVE – A document that spells out a specific directive of what you want to happen should a situation arise involving life-sustaining treatment. This document does not rely on the actions of another individual; rather, it gives the instructions directly to the doctor and medical staff.

IMMEDIATE ANNUITY – An agreement between you and an insurance company whereby the income payments start immediately, providing a set amount of income for an established period such as 20 years or an individual's lifetime.

INDEXED ANNUITY – A flexible insurance tool that uses an indexing method to give you market-linked gains without direct exposure to market risk, with the option for income at some future date.

INFLATION – The general rate at which the price of goods and services gradually rises.

INVESTMENT PLAN – A method for investing and saving money during your working years with a focus on making money.

INTEREST RATE RISK – The potential for loss when interest rates change, usually in reference to the value of bonds or other fixed-income investments.

LEGACY RATE – The minimum interest rate your portfolio needs to earn to offset the RMD and allow for an ample legacy for your beneficiaries.

LIQUIDITY – How quickly or easily you can convert an asset into cash.

MATH OF REBOUNDS – The mathematical calculation that tells us how much of a return we need to generate to recover from a period of negative activity or loss.

PRINCIPAL – The base amount of money that you put into an investment.

PRESERVATION RATE – The minimum interest rate your portfolio needs to earn to allow for regular spending without any loss of principal.

PROBATE – The sometimes costly and lengthy legal process by which the assets of the deceased are properly distributed, the objective being to ensure that the deceased's debts, taxes, and other valid claims are paid out of their estate so the assets are distributed to the intended beneficiaries.

RISK – The danger or probability of loss.

REQUIRED MINIMUM DISTRIBUTION (RMD) – The minimum amount you must withdraw from qualified retirement accounts such as a traditional IRA by April 1 following the year you reach age 70 ½ or age 72.

RETIREMENT PLAN – A written document designed to get you through your distribution years by illustrating the amount and duration of your retirement income and addressing the areas of investment efficiency, taxation, healthcare, and legacy planning.

RETIREMENT RED ZONE – The years just before and just after your time of retirement when your assets are most vulnerable to sequence risk.

ROTH IRA – Individual retirement arrangement made with income after the taxes have been paid where designated funds can grow tax-free with no taxes due on the interest earned if the withdrawal rules are followed.

SAFE MONEY – A term used by advisors to refer to financial vehicles that guarantee your principal and do not carry a risk of loss across all types of market cycles.

SEQUENCE RISK – A risk created by the order or sequence of market returns once withdrawals are coming out of an investment portfolio.

SPEND DOWN RATE – The minimum interest rate your portfolio needs to earn to keep your account healthy for a specific period of time that, when over, would result in a zero account balance.

SURRENDER CHARGE – A penalty charged to an investor for taking the money out of an insurance or annuity contract early.

TRADITIONAL IRA – An individual retirement arrangement that provides a way to set aside money for retirement using contributions that are subtracted from your income (reducing the income taxes owed) and allowed to grow tax-free until the money is withdrawn, at which point taxes are owed on both the principal and interest earned.

TRUST – A legal document that creates an entity that is separate from you designed to hold the title to assets while following a specific set of instructions for the management and distribution of those assets.

VARIABLE ANNUITY – A type of deferred annuity with income features where assets are held inside mutual funds invested in the stock market with the potential to earn returns and lose principal due to market loss.

VOLATILITY – A measure of the size and frequency of the change in stock market prices.

WITHDRAWAL WORKSHEET – The part of your written retirement plan that projects how much income you'll receive every month, how much the account is projected to earn, and when or if the money will run out.